THEMES ON THE JOURNEY

THEMES ON THE JOURNEY

REFLECTIONS IN POETRY

EDITED BY JAMES BARRY

Brebeuf College School

NelsonCanada

Published in 1989 by
Nelson Canada,
A Division of International Thomson Limited
1120 Birchmount Road
Scarborough, Ontario
M1K 5G4

ISBN 0-17-603089-1

Canadian Cataloguing in Publication Data
Main entry under title:

Themes on the journey

Includes index.
ISBN 0-17-603-089-1

1. Canadian poetry (English).* 2. American poetry.
3. English poetry. I. Barry, James, 1939– .

PN610.T48 1989   C811'.008   C89-093263-8

Project Manager: David Friend
Art Direction: Lorraine Tuson
Design: David Drummond and Gail McGowan
Cover Design: Gail McGowan
Cover Illustration: Stephan Daigle
Typesetting: HyperImage Inc.
Printing: Gagne Printing Ltd.

Printed and Bound in Canada
67890/ /8765432

TABLE OF CONTENTS

THEMES ON THE JOURNEY

TABLE OF CONTENTS

TABLE OF CONTENTS

TABLE OF CONTENTS

TABLE OF CONTENTS

TABLE OF CONTENTS

TABLE OF CONTENTS

TABLE OF CONTENTS

TABLE OF CONTENTS

TABLE OF CONTENTS

This Book Is about Poetry, Poets, and You.

U2

There was a time when all the colours didn't bleed into one. There was a time when evening didn't hold the bones of day. There was a time when an agèd man wasn't a paltry thing, a tattered coat upon a stick, and there was a time when life wasn't a poor player strutting and fretting his hour upon the stage.

COCKBURN

But then there was poetry, and blue-bleak embers would fall and gash themselves gold-vermilion. And hollow stuffed men filled with straw would lean together and the stars would throw down their spears and water heaven with their tears.

YEATS

The schemes of mice and men all went wrong.
And a narrow wind complained all day.
The rain was the feathery fringe of a shawl,
And love was like falling glass shaking with stars.

SHAKESPEARE

And with poetry came
the farms forever fled from the childless lands
and the sun rising dripping a bucketful of gold
and the ruby flare of an ambulance pulsing out light

and the poems for the intellectuals
and the poems for the real people,
hard-knuckled, ecstatic in odd syntax
and flashing barbs of truth and joy and hurt.

HOPKINS

These are the words of some of the poets in this book.

ELIOT

We are better people, richer folk because they jotted down their feelings, experiences, opinions, delights, and sorrows in words.

Come along. Walk with some words. Read some poems. Poetry won't go away.

BURNS

DICKINSON   LIVESAY   WEBB   THOMAS   MILLAY   SHAPIRO   DUDEK

•• THEME   = the meaning, the point, the gist, the essence
JOURNEY   = the human journey
                a poetic documentary in 82 parts

How to Read Poetry

With a wary eye, an expansive mind, a hungry heart, and open palms.

A poem is a small word machine that speaks to different individuals in different ways.

However, although the poem is created afresh each time it is read, the poem does rest on a textual base. It may mean more than one or two or even three things, but it doesn't mean all and anything.

Poems should be read and experienced from more than the vague, "anything-goes" subjective viewpoint. Textual evidence and verification are vital.

The reader embarks on the constant search for the feeling, the thought, the inspiration, the clarification that the poet has couched, cradled, packaged, bundled in the best words in their most appropriate form.

I write half the poem. The reader writes the other half.
                                Paul Valéry

The Mother's Song

It is so still in the house
The snowstorm wails out there,
And the dogs are rolled up with snouts under the tail.
My little boy is sleeping on the ledge,
On his back he lives, breathing through his open mouth
His little stomach is bulging round —
Is it strange if I start to cry with joy?

traditional Inuit song

Motherhood

Her eyes were shining brightly
A glow was stretched
around her skin-tight face

She laughed out brashly
when they said
"You've had a boy"

A boy? she queried wildly—
(as though the specie
had a dozen kinds)

A boy... a boy?
She laughed again in wonder

But when they placed him
in her arms
　　she cried
　　and cried
　　and cried!

Theresa Lewis

My Papa's Waltz

The whiskey on your breath
Could make a small boy dizzy;
But I hung on like death:
Such waltzing was not easy.

We romped until the pans
Slid from the kitchen shelf;
My mother's countenance
Could not unfrown itself.

The hand that held my wrist
Was battered on one knuckle;
At every step you missed
My right ear scraped a buckle.

You beat time on my head
With a palm caked hard by dirt,
Then waltzed me off to bed
Still clinging to your shirt.

Theodore Roethke

Fern Hill

Now as I was young and easy under the apple boughs
About the lilting house and happy as the grass was green,
    The night above the dingle starry,
      Time let me hail and climb
    Golden in the heydays of his eyes,
And honoured among wagons I was prince of the apple towns
And once below a time I lordly had the trees and leaves
      Trail with daisies and barley
    Down the rivers of the windfall light.   9

And as I was green and carefree, famous among the barns
About the happy yard and singing as the farm was home,
    In the sun that is young once only,
      Time let me play and be
    Golden in the mercy of his means,
And green and golden I was huntsman and herdsman, the calves
Sang to my horn, the foxes on the hills barked clear and cold,
      And the sabbath rang slowly
    In the pebbles of the holy streams.   18

All the sun long it was running, it was lovely, the hay-
Fields high as the house, the tunes from the chimneys, it was air
    And playing, lovely and watery
      And fire green as grass.
    And nightly under the simple stars
As I rode to sleep the owls were bearing the farm away,
All the moon long I heard, blessed among stables, the nightjars
    Flying with the ricks, and horses
      Flashing into the dark.   27

And then to awake, and the farm, like a wanderer white
With the dew, come back, the cock on his shoulder: it was all
    Shining, it was Adam and maiden,
      The sky gathered again
    And the sun grew round that very day.
So it must have been after the birth of the simple light
In the first, spinning place, the spellbound horses walking warm
    Out of the whinnying green stable
      On to the fields of praise.   36

And honoured among foxes and pheasants by the gay house
Under the newmade clouds and happy as the heart was long,
   In the sun born over and over,
     I ran my heedless ways,
   My wishes raced through the house-high hay
And nothing I cared, at my sky blue trades, that time allows
In all his tuneful turning so few and such morning songs
   Before the children green and golden
     Follow him out of grace,   45

Nothing I cared, in the lamb white days, that time would take me
Up to the swallow-thronged loft by the shadow of my hand,
   In the moon that is always rising,
     Nor that riding to sleep
   I should hear him fly with the high fields
And wake to the farm forever fled from the childless land.
Oh as I was young and easy in the mercy of his means,
     Time held me green and dying
     Though I sang in my chains like the sea.   54

Dylan Thomas

Dream Three: The Child

He was turning and turning and turning and turning
outside my window on a big unicycle
suspended in air beside a black tree.

Hey, why are you turning and turning and turning
getting nowhere fast on that wheel
when you could be talking to me?

I've always been here, turning and turning
and I'll always be here, turning and turning,
from the beginning and to the end turning,
from alpha to omega turning and turning,
and I looked and saw it was me.

Gwendolyn MacEwen

First Ice

A girl freezes in a telephone booth.
In her draughty overcoat she hides
A face all smeared
In tears and lipstick.

She breathes on her thin palms.
Her fingers are icy. She wears earrings.

She'll have to go home alone, alone,
Along the icy street.

First ice. It is the first time.
The first ice of telephone phrases.

Frozen tears glitter on her cheeks—
The first ice of human hurt.

Translated from the Russian by George Reavey

Andrei Voznesensky

Young

A thousand doors ago
when I was a lonely kid
in a big house with four
garages and it was summer
as long as I could remember,
I lay on the lawn at night
clover wrinkling under me,
my mother's window a funnel
of yellow heat running out,
my father's window, half shut,
an eye where sleepers pass,
and the boards of the house
were smooth and white as wax
and probably a million leaves
sailed on their strange stalks
as the crickets ticked together,
and I, in my brand new body,
which was not a woman's yet,
told the stars my questions
and thought God could really see
the heat and the painted light,
elbows, knees, dreams, goodnight.

Anne Sexton

Mother to Son

Well, son, I'll tell you:
Life for me ain't been no crystal stair.
It's had tacks in it,
And splinters,
And boards torn up,
And places with no carpet on the floor—
Bare.
But all the time
I'se been a-climbin' on,
And reachin' landin's,
And turnin' corners,
And sometimes goin' in the dark
Where there ain't been no light.
So, boy, don't you turn back.
Don't you set down on the steps
'Cause you finds it kinder hard.
Don't you fall now—
For I'se still goin', honey,
I'se still climbin',
And life for me ain't been no crystal stair.

Langston Hughes

Spring

Nothing is so beautiful as spring—
When weeds, in wheels, shoot long and lovely and lush;
Thrush's eggs look little low heavens, and thrush
Through the echoing timber does so rinse and wring
The ear, it strikes like lightning to hear him sing;
The glassy peartree leaves and blooms, they brush
The descending blue; that blue is all in a rush
With richness; the racing lambs too have fair their fling.

What is all this juice and all this joy?
A strain of the earth's sweet being in the beginning
In Eden Garden. — Have, get, before it cloy,
Before it cloud, Christ, lord, and sour with sinning,
Innocent mind and Mayday in girl and boy,
Most, O maid's child, thy choice and worthy the winning.

Gerard Manley Hopkins

She Loves Me

Emmett Williams

O My Luve's Like a Red, Red Rose

O my Luve's like a red, red rose
 That's newly sprung in June;
O my Luve's like the melodie
 That's sweetly play'd in tune.

As fair art thou, my bonnie lass,
 So deep in luve am I;
And I will luve thee still, my dear,
 Till a' the seas gang dry.

Till a' the seas gang dry, my dear,
 And the rocks melt wi' the sun;
I will luve thee still, my dear,
 While the sands o'life shall run.

And fare thee well, my only Luve!
 And fare thee well a while!
And I will come again, my Luve,
 Tho' it were ten thousand mile.

Robert Burns

Interpretation is the revenge of the intellect upon art.

Susan Sontag

The Masks of Love

I come in from a walk
with you
and they ask me
if it is raining.

I didn't notice
but I'll have to give them
the right answer
or they'll think I'm crazy.

Alden Nowlan

Blues

bpNichol

For Anne

With Annie gone,
whose eyes to compare
with the morning sun?

Not that I did compare,
But I do compare
Now that she's gone.

Leonard Cohen

How Do I Love Thee

How do I love thee? Let me count the ways.
I love thee to the depth and breadth and height
My soul can reach, when feeling out of sight
For the ends of Being and ideal Grace.
I love thee to the level of every day's
Most quiet need, by sun and candlelight.
I love thee freely, as men strive for Right;
I love thee purely, as they turn from Praise;
I love thee with the passion put to use
In my old griefs, and with my childhood's faith;
I love thee with a love I seemed to lose
With my lost saints,—I love thee with the breath,
Smiles, tears, of all my life!—and, if God choose,
I shall but love thee better after death.

Elizabeth Barrett Browning

found lipprints
in the snow
by your door
wish you'd stop
kissing his feet

Jillian Millar

Recuerdo

We were very tired, we were very merry—
We had gone back and forth all night on the ferry.
It was bare and bright, and smelled like a stable—
But we looked into a fire, we leaned across a table,
We lay on a hill-top underneath the moon;
And the whistles kept blowing, and the dawn came soon.

We were very tired, we were very merry—
We had gone back and forth all night on the ferry;
And you ate an apple, and I ate a pear,
From a dozen of each we had bought somewhere;
And the sky went wan, and the wind came cold,
And the sun rose dripping, a bucketful of gold.

We were very tired, we were very merry,
We had gone back and forth all night on the ferry.
We hailed, "Good morrow, mother!" to a shawl-covered head,
And bought a morning paper, which neither of us read;
And she wept, "God bless you!" for the apples and pears
And we gave her all our money but our subway fares.

Edna St. Vincent Millay

a nyone lived in a pretty how town

anyone lived in a pretty how town ·
(with up so floating many bells down)
spring summer autumn winter
he sang his didn't he danced his did.

Women and men (both little and small)
cared for anyone not at all
they sowed their isn't they reaped their same
sun moon stars rain

children guessed (but only a few
and down they forgot as up they grew
autumn winter spring summer)
that noone loved him more by more

when by now and tree by leaf
she laughed his joy she cried his grief
bird by snow and stir by still
anyone's any was all to her

someones married their everyones
laughed their cryings and did their dance
(sleep wake hope then) they
said their nevers they slept their dream

stars rain sun moon
(and only the snow can begin to explain
how children are apt to forget to remember
with up so floating many bells down)

one day anyone died i guess
(and noone stooped to kiss his face)
busy folk buried them side by side
little by little and was by was

all by all and deep by deep
and more by more they dream their sleep
noone and anyone earth by april
wish by spirit and if by yes.

Women and men (both dong and ding)
summer autumn winter spring
reaped their sowing and went their came
sun moon stars rain

e. e. cummings

• • When you write a poem, you touch the person that you really are.
When you write a poem, you share something of yourself with others.
When you write a poem, you are alone with your own existence.

1, Icarus

There was a time when I could fly. I swear it.
Perhaps, if I think hard for a moment, I can even tell you the year.
My room was on the ground floor at the rear of the house.
My bed faced a window.
Night after night I lay on my bed and willed myself to fly.
It was hard work, I can tell you.
Sometimes I lay perfectly still for an hour before I felt
    my body rising from the bed.
I rose slowly, slowly until I floated three or four feet
    above the floor.
Then, with a kind of swimming motion, I propelled myself
    toward the window.
Outside, I rose higher and higher, above the pasture fence,
    above the clothesline, above the dark, haunted trees
    beyond the pasture.
And, all the time, I heard the music of flutes.
It seemed the wind made this music.
And sometimes there were voices singing.

Alden Nowlan

Flight of the Roller-Coaster

Once more around should do it, the man confided...

and, sure enough, when the roller-coaster reached the peak
of the giant curve above me, screech of its wheels
almost drowned out by the shriller cries of the riders,

instead of the dip and plunge with its landslide of screams,
it rose in the air like a movieland magic carpet,
    some wonderful bird,

and without fuss or fanfare swooped slowly across
    the amusement-park,
over Spook's Castle, ice-cream booths, shooting-gallery.
    And losing no height

made the last yards above the beach, where the cucumber-cool
brakeman in the last seat saluted
a lady about to change from her bathing-suit.

Then, as many witnesses reported, headed leisurely
    out over the water,
disappearing all too soon behind a low-flying flight of clouds.

Raymond Souster

On First Looking into Chapman's Homer

Much have I travelled in the realms of gold,
    And many goodly states and kingdoms seen;
    Round many western islands have I been
Which bards in fealty to Apollo hold.
Oft of one wide expanse had I been told
    That deep-browed Homer ruled as his demesne;
    Yet did I never breathe its pure serene
Till I heard Chapman speak out loud and bold:
Then felt I like some watcher of the skies
    When a new planet swims into his ken;
Or like stout Cortez when with eagle eyes
    He stared at the Pacific—and all his men
Looked at each other with a wild surmise—
    Silent, upon a peak in Darien.

John Keats

Song of Perfect Propriety

Oh, I should like to ride the seas,
A roaring buccaneer;
A cutlass banging at my knees,
A dirk behind my ear.
And when my captives' chains would clank
I'd howl with glee and drink,
And then fling out the quivering plank
And watch the beggars sink.

I'd like to straddle gory decks,
And dig in laden sands,
And know the feel of throbbing necks
Between my knotted hands.
Oh, I should like to strut and curse
Among my blackguard crew…
But I am writing little verse,
As little ladies do.

Oh, I should like to dance and laugh
And pose and preen and sway,
And rip the hearts of men in half,
And toss the bits away.
I'd like to view the reeling years
Through unastonished eyes,
And dip my finger-tips in tears,
And give my smiles for sighs.

I'd stroll beyond the ancient bounds,
And tap at fastened gates,
And hear the prettiest of sounds—
The clink of shattered fates.
My slaves I'd like to bind with thongs
That cut and burn and chill…
But I am writing little songs,
As little ladies will.

Dorothy Parker

Dream Deferred

What happens to a dream deferred?

Does it dry up
like a raisin in the sun?
Or fester like a sore—
And then run?
Does it stink like rotten meat?
Or crust and sugar over—
like a syrupy sweet?

Maybe it just sags
like a heavy load.

Or does it explode?

Langston Hughes

The Night-March

With banners furled, and clarions mute,
    An army passes in the night;
And beaming spears and helms salute
    The dark with bright.

In silence deep the legions stream,
    With open ranks, in order true;
Over boundless plains they stream and gleam—
    No chief in view!

Afar, in twinkling distance lost,
    (So legends tell) he lonely wends
And back through all that shining host
    His mandate sends.

Herman Melville

Another Night with Telescope

Come back to me
            brutal empty room
Thin Byzantine face
        preside over this new fast
I am broken with easy grace
Let me be neither
            father nor child
but one who spins
on an eternal unimportant loom
        patterns of wars and grass
which do not last the night
            I know the stars
are wild as dust
and wait for no man's discipline
            but as they wheel
from sky to sky they rake
        our lives with pins of light

Leonard Cohen

Sea Gull

Something sacred he seems
raised for worship
above the grey sea altar

poised on priest wind hands
he awaits
the genuflection

a certain concern for eternity
kneels me on the salt wet rock
and seeming satisfied
with that small penance
he tips one wing in casual benediction
and moves on seaward
to command another's adoration

Al Pittman

"The seagull, swimsuit of God."

Andrei Voznesensky

Sea-Gulls

For one carved instant as they flew,
The language had no simile—
Silver, crystal, ivory
Were tarnished. Etched upon the horizon blue,
The frieze must go unchallenged, for the lift
And carriage of the wings would stain the drift
Of stars against a tropic indigo
Or dull the parable of snow.
Now settling one by one
Within green hollows or where curled
Crests caught the spectrum from the sun,
A thousand wings are furled.
No clay-born lilies of the world
Could blow as free
As those wild orchids of the sea.

E. J. Pratt

Sun Poem

The sun
a peeping Tom
got his eyelids
thru the window
and brushed my desert brow.

I leaped
from the grave of a bed
and bolted the venetian blinds down
like guillotine.
Part of his eyelids fell on the floor.
I'll sweep them up soon.

Joe Rosenblatt

Dave's Fall

In fall I see stained glass sky
and elm trees like arches
in an abandoned cathedral.
　　Dave says he hears orange sound.
I can only imagine,
Maybe it's the sound of an absent wind
no longer brushing against fallen leaves
that lie crisp in dusty sunlight,
　　but he can't see the sunlight,
only hears orange sound
as his white cane
sweeps through the leaves.

Andrea Holtslander

The Sky is low—the Clouds are mean.
A Travelling Flake of Snow
Across a Barn or through a Rut
Debates if it will go—

A Narrow Wind complains all Day
How some one treated him
Nature, like Us is sometimes caught
Without her Diadem.

Emily Dickinson

Art's single greatest potential is - surprise.

Guillaume Apollinaire

33

I like to see it lap the Miles—
And lick the Valleys up—
And stop to feed itself at Tanks—
And then—prodigious step

Around a Pile of Mountains—
And supercilious peer
In Shanties—by the sides of Roads—
And then a Quarry pare

To fit its Ribs
And crawl between
Complaining all the while
In horrid—hooting stanza—
Then chase itself down Hill—

And neigh like Boanerges—
Then—punctual as a Star
Stop—docile and omnipotent
At its own stable door—

Emily Dickinson

Tree in a Street

Why will not that tree adapt itself to our tempo?
We have lopped off several branches,
cut her skin to the white bone,
run wires through her body and her loins,
yet she will not change.
Ignorant of traffic, of dynamos and steel,
as uncontemporary
as bloomers and bustles
she stands there like a green cliché.

Louis Dudek

Earth

"A planet doesn't explode of itself," said drily
The Martian astronomer, gazing off into the air—
"That they were able to do it is proof that highly
Intelligent beings must have been living there."

John Hall Wheelock

On Samsonite Assembly Line 72

riveting suitcases

Rivet a blue one, rivet a blue one, rivet a blue one, rivet
a blue one, rivet a blue one, rivet a blue one, rivet a blue
one, rivet a blue one, rivet a blue one, rivet a blue one
    rivet a blue one   rivet a blue one
     rivet a blue one   rivet a blue one
    rivet a blue one rivet blue rivet one a blue blue blue
        THANK GOD A RED ONE!
    rivet a blue one rivet a blue one rivet one hundred rivet
an hour rivet rivet blue rivet suitcases rivet rivet wait rivet
for rivet coffee rivet rivet break

Rich Duquet

God's Grandeur

The world is charged with the grandeur of God.
  It will flame out, like shining from shook foil;
  It gathers to a greatness, like the ooze of oil
Crushed. Why do men then now not reck his rod?
Generations have trod, have trod, have trod;
  And all is seared with trade; bleared, smeared with toil;
  And wears man's smudge and shares man's smell: the soil
Is bare now, nor can foot feel, being shod.

And for all this, nature is never spent;
  There lives the dearest freshness deep down things;
And though the last lights off the black West went
  Oh, morning, at the brown brink eastward, springs—
Because the Holy Ghost over the bent
  World broods with warm breast and with ah! bright wings.

Gerard Manley Hopkins

uto Wreck

Its quick soft silver bell beating, beating;
And down the dark one ruby flare
Pulsing out red light like an artery,
The ambulance at top speed floating down
Past beacons and illuminated clocks
Wings in a heavy curve, dips down,
And brakes speed, entering the crowd.
The doors leap open, emptying light;
Stretchers are laid out, the mangled lifted
And stowed into the little hospital.   10
Then the bell, breaking the hush, tolls once,
And the ambulance with its terrible cargo
Rocking, slightly rocking, moves away,
As the doors, an afterthought, are closed.

We are deranged, walking among the cops
Who sweep glass and are large and composed.
One is still making notes under the light.
One with a bucket douches ponds of blood
Into the street and gutter.
One hangs lanterns on the wrecks that cling,   20
Empty husks of locusts, to iron poles.

Our throats were tight as tourniquets,
Our feet were bound with splints, but now,
Like convalescents intimate and gauche,
We speak through sickly smiles and warn
With the stubborn saw of common sense,
The grim joke and the banal resolution.
The traffic moves around with care,
But we remain, touching a wound
That opens to our richest horror.   30
Already old, the question Who shall die?
Becomes unspoken Who is innocent?

For death in war is done by hands;
Suicide has cause and stillbirth, logic;
And cancer, simple as a flower, blooms.
But this invites the occult mind,
Cancels our physics with a sneer,
And spatters all we knew of denouement
Across the expedient and wicked stones.

Karl Shapiro

Last Ride

We watch in horror as
the booster rockets twist
crazily through the sky
like balloons
whipped free
from a child's grasp.

The horror is the reality on the screen.

"On this day of tragedy…we watch in horror
as…"
   And for the benefit of those who
missed the live show
      we will run the
       fireworks once again.

   The spotlight moves to the grief-stricken
families and we can have our
        heart-strings pulled
    with 20 million others
as we watch their
tears fall,
    LIVE.

   Having wrung all the tears from his
audience the ringmaster can now turn to sports
       as seven families try to put
    together their lives
       scattered over the Atlantic
        Ocean.

Andrea Holtslander

Death by Streetcar

The old lady crushed to death by the Bathurst streetcar
had one cent left in her purse when they found her.
Which could mean only one of two things:
either she was very wary of purse-snatchers,
or else all her money was gone.
     If the latter,
she must have known her luck would very soon change
for better or for worse. Which this day has decided.

Raymond Souster

the miserable man
i treat you as a stranger....
you were born and reared in
                        squalor...
you are walled in, for you have
                        no life
in front of you.....no joys to
                        look
forward to....no loving
                        children....
no esteem

t
w
o

p
r
i
s
o
n
s

d
i
v
i
d
e
d

b
y

a

g
u
l
f

i, with my clean clothes, my
sensitive nose (i hate bad
smells)
my politeness....a warm
house...
a world of security...the light
of reality does not penetrate my
cell, the reality of human
misery
so widespread, so deep.....

two prisons divided by a gulf: the miserable
                        man......
and, imprisoned in the cell next door, the man
                        of means
comfortably installed.....and so the world
                        goes on,
and the gulf gets wider

who will be the bridge

Jean Vanier

The Old Convict

Look at me. I am Ishmael,
 Ham's heir, the spit and spawn of Cain,
 The outcast with the twisted brain,
Lord of Cats Castle, fit for Hell.

I got no chance. The social odds
 Were dead against me when they sent
 Me up The Hill because I went
For some forgotten prank to Dodds.

And so because they made me wince,
 And stretched me on the legal rack,
 I took an oath I would hit back,
And have been hitting ever since.

Maybe it *is* a foolish game
 Judged by the record. Who likes jail?
 But then I've fought them tooth and nail,
And surely that's no cause for shame.

Reform, you say? Reform indeed!
 Let's all reform. They must not quit
 The Golden Rule, and I from it
Will not stray once. That is our need.

H. A. Vaughan

```
sem    um    numero
       um    numero
             numero
                mero
                 um
                  o
                 nu
                mero
             numero
       um    numero
       um  sem  numero
```

Augusto de Campos

> He is a poet because his interest in experience
> is not separable from his interest in words.
>
> **F.R. Leavis**

Ex-basketball Player

Pearl Avenue runs past the high-school lot,
Bends with the trolley tracks, and stops, cut off
Before it has a chance to go two blocks,
At Colonel McComsky Plaza. Berth's Garage
Is on the corner facing west, and there,
Most days, you'll find Flick Webb, who helps Berth out.

Flick stands tall among the idiot pumps—
Five on a side, the old bubble-head style,
Their rubber elbows hanging loose and low.
One's nostrils are two S's, and his eyes
An E and O. And one is squat, without
A head at all—more of a football type.

Once Flick played for the high-school team, the Wizards.
He was good: in fact, the best. In '46
He bucketed three hundred ninety points,
A county record still. The ball loved Flick.
I saw him rack up thirty-eight or forty
In one home game. His hands were like wild birds.

He never learned a trade, he just sells gas,
Checks oil, and changes flats. Once in a while,
As a gag, he dribbles an inner tube,
But most of us remember anyway.
His hands are fine and nervous on the lug wrench.
It makes no difference to the lug wrench, though.

Off work, he hangs around Mae's Luncheonette.
Grease-grey and kind of coiled, he plays pinball,
Sips lemon cokes, and smokes those thin cigars;
Flick seldom speaks to Mae, just sits and nods
Beyond her face towards bright applauding tiers
Of Necco Wafers, Nibs, and Juju Beads.

John Updike

Identity

I
Ever-broken
Identity
The knot begins to feel
The cord it is made of turn

II
The strange beating of one's heart
Reaches one through the fog
One hears it
What an odd time-piece

A room with furnishings
The time-piece on the table
All this is part of the room
One looks through the windows
One comes to sit at one's desk
One works
One rests
Everything is calm

Suddenly: tick tock
The wall clock reaches one's ears
And worries its way to one's ears
Softly it comes
To break all the room into bits

One raises one's eyes: a ghost has moved the mantelpiece
A ghost pushes the mantelpiece
The furniture is all changed

And when everything begins to exist on its own
Each unfamiliar piece
Begins to contradict the other

Where is it one stays
Where does one live
Everything is in holes and pieces

Translated from the French by Fred Cogswell

Hector de Saint-Denys Garneau

The Red Cockatoo

Sent as a present from Annam—
A red cockatoo.
Coloured like the peach-tree
    blossom,
Speaking with the speech of men.
And they did to it what is always
    done
To the learned and eloquent.
They took a cage with stout bars
And shut it up inside.

紅鸚鵡 _{商山路逢}

安南遠進紅鸚鵡。色似桃花語似人。文章辯慧皆如此。籠檻何年出得身。

Po Chü-I

To Hold in a Poem

I would take words
As crisp and as white
As our snow; as our birds
Swift and sure in their flight;

As clear and as cold
As our ice; as strong as a jack pine;
As young as a trillium, and old
As Laurentia's long undulant line;

Sweet-smelling and bright
As new rain; as hard
And as smooth and as white
As a brook pebble cold and unmarred;

To hold in a poem of words
Like water in colourless glass
The spirit of mountains like birds,
Of forests as pointed as grass;

To hold in a verse as austere
As the spirit of prairie and river,
Lonely, unbuyable, dear,
The North, as a deed, and forever.

A. J. M. Smith

Poetry for Intellectuals

If you say in a poem "grass is green,"
They all ask, "What did you mean?"

"That nature is ignorant," you reply;
"On a deeper 'level'—youth must die."

If you say in a poem "grass is red,"
They understand what you have said.

Louis Dudek

The Garden of the Thieves

For years I have wanted to write a poem called
        The Garden of the Thieves.
The title turns up in old notebooks with asterisks
Surrounding it and arrows pointing to it, and
Notes telling me to write it, write it, but

It never got written until now because I never knew
        where the garden was, or who
The thieves were, so the naked title lay there
Between sheets of paper that seethed with reason
And grand ideas, until one night I actually dreamed

Of the garden where I played as a child, and it was
        invaded by *thieves*
Who stole the Great Poem from me, the one we all know
Never gets written, and I saw the title as they
Whisked it away, and yes, it was beyond a doubt

The Garden of the Thieves, written by Anonymous
        who was my favourite poet
And who I thought was a Byzantine king. I have been
Pondering over this for quite some time, and thought
I'd better get it all down before the night falls.

Gwendolyn MacEwen

This Is a Photograph of Me

It was taken some time ago.
At first it seems to be
a smeared
print: blurred lines and grey flecks
blended with the paper;

then, as you scan
it, you see in the left-hand corner
a thing that is like a branch: part of a tree
(balsam or spruce) emerging
and, to the right, halfway up
what ought to be a gentle
slope, a small frame house.

In the background there is a lake,
and beyond that, some low hills.

(The photograph was taken
the day after I drowned.

I am in the lake, in the centre
of the picture, just under the surface.

It is difficult to say where
precisely, or to say
how large or small I am:
the effect of water
on light is a distortion

but if you look long enough,
eventually
you will be able to see me.)

Margaret Atwood

*Images in verse are not mere decoration, but the
very essence of an intuitive language.*

T.E. Hulme

Mirror

I am silver and exact. I have no preconceptions.
Whatever I see I swallow immediately
Just as it is, unmisted by love or dislike.
I am not cruel, only truthful—
The eye of a little god, four-cornered.
Most of the time I meditate on the opposite wall.
It is pink, with speckles. I have looked at it so long
I think it is a part of my heart. But it flickers.
Faces and darkness separate us over and over.

Now I am a lake. A woman bends over me,
Searching my reaches for what she really is.
Then she turns to those liars, the candles or the moon.
I see her back, and reflect it faithfully.
She rewards me with tears and an agitation of hands.
I am important to her. She comes and goes.
Each morning it is her face that replaces the darkness.
In me she has drowned a young girl, and in me an old woman
Rises toward her day after day, like a terrible fish.

Sylvia Plath

The Blue

The Bow River
was blue today,
the sky,
the Rockies somewhere

that is, the mud
has sunk,
the ice
disappeared sometime.

I would do that,
disappear sometime
like a blue river
on the prairie.

George Bowering

I'm talking about the smallish, unofficial garden-variety poem. How shall I describe it?— a door opens, a door shuts.

Sylvia Plath

Canada: Case History

This is the case of a highschool land
deadset in adolescence
loud treble laughs and sudden fists
bright cheeks   the gangling presence
This boy is oriented well to sports
and the doctors say he's healthy
he's taken to church on Sunday still
and keeps his prurience stealthy
Doesn't like books (except about bears)
collects new coins   old slogans   jets
and never refuses a dare
His Uncle spoils him with candy of course
but shouts him down when he talks at table
You'll note he has some of his French mother's looks
though he's not so witty and no more stable
He's really much more like his Father and yet
if you say so he'll pull a great face
He wants to be different from everyone else
and daydreams of winning the global race
Parents unmarried and living apart
relatives keen to bag the estate
schizophrenia not excluded—
will he learn to grow up before it's too late?

Earle Birney

Islanders

Would you guess from their broad greeting,
witty tuck of eyelids,
how they putt-putt out with lunch-cans
on sea liable to tangle
and dim out the land between two glances?

Tho their dads toed the decks of schooners,
dodging the blustery rush of capes,
and rum-runner uncles used wit-grease
against the shoot-first Yankee cutters,
they wouldn't be the kind to sail their
                    lobster boats around the world
for anything less than a dollar-ninety an hour.

Milton Acorn

Transformations

The blood of my ancestors
has died in me
I have forsaken the steppes
of Russia for the prairies
of Winnipeg, I have turned
my back on Minneapolis
and the Detroit lakes
I love only St. Boniface
its grey wooden churches
I want to spend my life
in Gimli listening to the
roar of emptiness in the
wild snow, scanning the lake
for the music of rainbow-
skinned fishes, I will compose
my songs to gold-eye tunes
send them across the land
in smoke-spaces, ice-signals
and concentrate all winter
on Henry Hudson adrift
in a boat, when he comes home
I will come home too and
the blood of my ancestors
will flower on Mennonite bushes

Miriam Waddington

Rush Hour Tokyo

Pelted shapeless in rush hour crush
As in a whash mash mochi making
A mad cab exhaust spot
Bicycle pedestrian car cart jostling
Hip to bumper, wheel to toe
Police whistle siren scream political
Speech radio singer neon I blur
Into this excess of faceless flesh rushing
Round this blender of glazed eyes—
Particle waves of people
Whip at typhoon speed past ticket takers
The world's most accurate mechanical men
And pummel up subway systems
Spew onto streets and platforms
Where demons within demons within demons
Riot for release or finale
Like staccato repetitions in frenzied fugues
Locked in a constant crescendo—
Canada oh my home and native land
Give me land lots of land don't
Fence don't fence me in—

Joy Kogawa

Laurentian Shield

Hidden in wonder and snow, or sudden with summer,
This land stares at the sun in a huge silence
Endlessly repeating something we cannot hear.
Inarticulate, arctic,
Not written on by history, empty as paper,
It leans away from the world with songs in its lakes
Older than love, and lost in the miles.

This waiting is wanting.
It will choose its language
When it has chosen its technic,   10
A tongue to shape the vowels of its productivity.

A language of flesh and of roses.

Now there are pre-words,
Cabin syllables,
Nouns of settlement
Slowly forming, with steel syntax,
The long sentence of its exploitation.

The first cry was the hunter, hungry for fur,
And the digger for gold, nomad, no-man, a particle;
Then the bold commands of monopoly, big with machines,   20
Carving its kingdoms out of the public wealth;
And now the drone of the plane, scouting the ice,
Fills all the emptiness with neighbourhood
And links our future over the vanished pole.

But a deeper note is sounding, heard in the mines,
The scattered camps and the mills, a language of life,
And what will be written in the full culture of occupation
Will come, presently, tomorrow,
From millions whose hands can turn this rock into children.

F. R. Scott

Poetry is nothing less than the most perfect speech of man, that in which he comes nearest to be able to utter the truth . . . .

Matthew Arnold

Dulce Et Decorum Est

Bent double, like old beggars under sacks,
Knock-kneed, coughing like hags, we cursed through sludge,
Till on the haunting flares we turned our backs,
And towards our distant rest began to trudge.
Men marched asleep. Many had lost their boots,
But limped on, blood-shod. All went lame, all blind;
Drunk with fatigue; deaf even to the hoots
Of gas-shells dropping softly behind.

Gas! GAS! Quick, boys!—An ecstasy of fumbling,
Fitting the clumsy helmets just in time,   10
But someone still was yelling out and stumbling
And flound'ring like a man in fire or lime.—
Dim through the misty panes and thick green light,
As under a green sea, I saw him drowning.

In all my dreams before my helpless sight
He plunges at me, guttering, choking, drowning.

If in some smothering dreams, you too could pace
Behind the wagon that we flung him in,
And watch the white eyes writhing in his face,
His hanging face, like a devil's sick of sin,   20
If you could hear, at every jolt, the blood
Come gargling from the froth-corrupted lungs
Bitter as the cud
Of vile, incurable sores on innocent tongues,—
My friend, you would not tell with such high zest
To children ardent for some desperate glory,
The old lie: *Dulce et decorum est*
Pro patria mori.

Wilfred Owen

The Anxious Dead

O guns, fall silent till the dead men hear
   Above their heads the legions pressing on:
(These fought their fight in time of bitter fear,
   And died not knowing how the day had gone.)

O flashing muzzles, pause, and let them see
   The coming dawn that streaks the sky afar;
Then let your mighty chorus witness be
   To them, and Caesar, that we still make war.

Tell them, O guns, that we have heard their call,
   That we have sworn, and will not turn aside,
That we will onward till we win or fall,
   That we will keep the faith for which they died.

Bid them be patient, and some day, anon,
   They shall feel earth enwrapt in silence deep;
Shall greet, in wonderment, the quiet dawn,
   And in content may turn them to their sleep.

John McCrae

Base Details

If I were fierce and bald and short of breath,
   I'd live with scarlet Majors at the Base,
And speed glum heroes up the line to death.
   You'd see me with my puffy petulant face,
Guzzling and gulping in the best hotel,
   Reading the Roll of Honour. "Poor young chap,"
I'd say—"I used to know his father well.
   Yes, we've lost heavily in this last scrap."
And when the war is done and youth stone dead,
   I'd toddle safely home and die—in bed.

Siegfried Sassoon

Fleet Fighter

"Good show!" he said, leaned his head back and laughed.
"They're wizard types!" he said, and held his beer
Steadily, looked at it and gulped it down
Out of its jam-jar, took a cigarette
And blew a neat smoke ring into the air.
"After this morning's prang I've got the twitch;
I thought I'd had it in that teased-out kite."
His eyes were blue, and older than his face,
His single stripe had known a lonely war
But all his talk and movements showed his age.
His whole life was the air and his machine,
He had no thought but of the latest "mod,"
His jargon was of aircraft or of beer.
"And what will you do afterwards?" I said,
Then saw his puzzled face, and caught my breath.
There was no afterwards for him, but death.

Olivia FitzRoy

A Page from Our History

Mackenzie King said,
"Conscription if necessary
but not necessarily conscription."

(So they took Steve in England,
on a signals course,
gave him one whole week
of infantry refresher,
then slipped him across
to the Hochwald where,
after three nightmare days
living mainly on rum,
an SS mortar
blew his left side off).

The historians now say
Mr. King saved Canada . . . .

As for Steve—
he gets a small pension,
and may learn in time
to walk without a cane.

Raymond Souster

Home

The people have got used to her
they have watched her children grow
and behave as if she were
one of them—how can they know
that every time she leaves her home
she is terrified of them
that as a German Jew she sees
them as potential enemies

Because she knows what has been done
to children who were like her own
she cannot think their future safe
her parents must have felt at home
where none cared what became of them
and as a child she must have played
with people who in later life
would have killed her had she stayed

Karen Gershon

The Death of the Ball Turret Gunner

From my mother's sleep I fell into the State,
And I hunched in its belly till my wet fur froze.
Six miles from earth, loosed from its dream of life,
I woke to black flak and the nightmare fighters.
When I died they washed me out of the turret with a hose.

Randall Jarrell

Hiroshima Exit

In round round rooms of our wanderings
Victims and victimizers in circular flight
Fact pursuing fact
Warning leaflets still drip down
On soil heavy with flames,
Black rain, footsteps, witnessings—

The Atomic Bomb Memorial Building:
A curiosity shop filled with
Remnants of clothing, radiation sickness,
Fleshless faces, tourists muttering
"Well, they started it."
Words jingle down
"They didn't think about us in Pearl Harbor"
They? Us?
I tiptoe round the curiosity shop
Seeking my target
Precision becomes essential
Quick. Quick. Before he's out of range
Spell the name
America?
Hiroshima?
Air raid warnings wail bleakly
Hiroshima
Morning.
I step outside
And close softly the door
Believing, believing
That outside this store
Is another door

Joy Kogawa

High Flight

Oh, I have slipped the surly bonds of earth
And danced the skies on laughter-silvered wings;
Sunward I've climbed and joined the tumbling mirth
Of sun-split clouds—and done a hundred things
You have not dreamed of—wheeled and soared and swung
High in the sunlit silence. Hov'ring there,
I've chased the shouting wind along and flung
My eager craft through footless halls of air.
Up, up the long delirious, burning blue
I've topped the wind-swept heights with easy grace,
Where never lark, or even eagle, flew;
And, while with silent, lifting mind I've trod
The high untrespassed sanctity of space,
Put out my hand and touched the face of God.

John Gillespie Magee

Highway 16/5 Illumination

South-east of Edmonton, on the road that leads
to Vermilion, Lloydminster, and the Saskatchewan border
I feel coming into me again like
a song about a man born in the country
the joy of the highway: the long road

that reaches ahead through these wooded rises, the farms
that spread their fields out around themselves
flat to the sun, the odour of hay filling the cabin of the car

mile by mile, border after border, horizon
to horizon. The highway stretches away
in all directions, linking and connecting
across an entire continent

and anywhere I point the front wheels
I can go.

Tom Wayman

The sky is the blue
Of the world's beginning—from my wife
I accept an apple.

Nakamura Kusatao

55

(fea
therr
ain

:dreamin
g field o
ver forest &;

wh
o could
be

so
!f!
te

r?n
oo
ne)

e. e. cummings

Stones in the Snow

To write a poem is
Finding stones in the snow—
Straining to see the nights,
Waiting to hear the winds,
Trying to smell the rain,
Stretching to touch the sun,
All these have turned
And borne them.
Snowflakes tasted are words
Which carry them.

Berenice B. Levchuk

The Great Sea

The great sea
Has sent me adrift,
It moves me as the weed in a great river,
Earth and the great weather
Move me,
Have carried me away
And move my inward parts with joy.

Uvavnuk

Keine Lazarovitch

1870-1959

When I saw my mother's head on the cold pillow,
Her white waterfalling hair in the cheeks' hollows,
I thought, quietly circling my grief, of how
She had loved God but cursed extravagantly his creatures.

For her final mouth was not water but a curse,
A small black hole, a black rent in the universe,
Which damned the green earth, stars and trees in its stillness
And the inescapable lousiness of growing old.

And I record she was comfortless, vituperative,
Ignorant, glad, and much else besides; I believe
She endlessly praised her black eyebrows, their thick weave,
Till plagiarizing Death leaned down and took them for his mould.

And spoiled a dignity I shall not again find,
And the fury of her stubborn limited mind;
Now none will shake her amber beads and call God blind,
Or wear them upon a breast so radiantly.

O fierce she was, mean and unaccommodating;
But I think now of the loss of her gold earrings,
Their proud carnal assertion, and her youngest sings
While all the rivers of her red veins move into the sea.

Irving Layton

The Philosophers

```
                    ladders
              park          then
              play
              high                  slide
         climb
        slowly                  laughing
        they
      while                      down
    nervously
  wave                            swift
Children                         years
```

R. G. Everson

Do Not Go Gentle into That Good Night

Do not go gentle into that good night,
Old age should burn and rave at close of day;
Rage, rage against the dying of the light.

Though wise men at their end know dark is right,
Because their words had forked no lightning they
Do not go gentle into that good night.

Good men, the last wave by, crying how bright
Their frail deeds might have danced in a green bay,
Rage, rage against the dying of the light.

Wild men who caught and sang the sun in flight,
And learn, too late, they grieved it on its way,
Do not go gentle into that good night.

Grave men, near death, who see with blinding sight
Blind eyes could blaze like meteors and be gay,
Rage, rage against the dying of the light.

And you, my father, there on the sad height,
Curse, bless, me now with your fierce tears, I pray.
Do not go gentle into that good night.
Rage, rage against the dying of the light.

Dylan Thomas

The best craftsmanship always leaves holes and gaps in the works of the poem so that what is not in the poem can creep, crawl, flash, or thunder in.

Dylan Thomas

On His Blindness

When I consider how my light is spent
Ere half my days in this dark world and wide,
And that one talent which is death to hide
Lodged with me useless, though my soul more bent
To serve therewith my Maker, and present
My true account, lest he returning chide,
"Doth God exact day-labour, light denied?"
I fondly ask. But Patience, to prevent
That murmur, soon replies, "God doth not need
Either man's work or his own gifts. Who best
Bear his mild yoke, they serve him best. His state
Is kingly: thousands at his bidding speed,
And post o'er land and ocean without rest;
They also serve who only stand and wait."

John Milton

Loveliest of Trees

Loveliest of trees, the cherry now
Is hung with bloom along the bough,
And stands about the woodland ride
Wearing white for Eastertide.

Now, of my threescore years and ten,
Twenty will not come again,
And take from seventy springs a score,
It only leaves me fifty more.

And since to look at things in bloom
Fifty springs are little room,
About the woodlands I will go
To see the cherry hung with snow.

A. E. Housman

Dover Beach

The sea is calm to-night.
The tide is full, the moon lies fair
Upon the straits;—on the French coast the light
Gleams and is gone; the cliffs of England stand
Glimmering and vast, out in the tranquil bay.

Come to the window, sweet is the night-air!
Only, from the long line of spray
Where the sea meets the moon-blanch'd land,
Listen! you hear the grating roar
Of pebbles which the waves draw back, and fling,   10
At their return, up the high strand,
Begin, and cease, and then again begin,
With tremulous cadence slow, and bring
The eternal note of sadness in.

Sophocles long ago
Heard it on the Ægean, and it brought
Into his mind the turbid ebb and flow,
Of human misery; we
Find also in the sound a thought,
Hearing it by this distant northern sea.   20

The Sea of Faith
Was once, too, at the full, and round earth's shore
Lay like the folds of a bright girdle furl'd.
But now I only hear
Its melancholy, long, withdrawing roar,
Retreating, to the breath
Of the night-wind, down the vast edges drear
And naked shingles of the world.

Ah, love, let us be true
To one another! for the world, which seems   30
To lie before us like a land of dreams,
So various, so beautiful, so new,
Hath really neither joy, nor love, nor light,
Nor certitude, nor peace, nor help for pain;
And we are here as on a darkling plain
Swept with confused alarms of struggle and flight,
Where ignorant armies clash by night.

Matthew Arnold

'Out, Out—'

The buzz saw snarled and rattled in the yard
And made dust and dropped stove-length sticks of wood,
Sweet-scented stuff when the breeze drew across it.
And from there those that lifted eyes could count
Five mountain ranges one behind the other
Under the sunset far into Vermont.
And the saw snarled and rattled, snarled and rattled,
As it ran light, or had to bear a load.
And nothing happened: day was all but done.
Call it a day, I wish they might have said   10
To please the boy by giving him the half hour
That a boy counts so much when saved from work.
His sister stood beside them in her apron
To tell them "Supper." At the word, the saw,
As if to prove saws knew what supper meant,
Leaped out at the boy's hand, or seemed to leap—
He must have given the hand. However it was,
Neither refused the meeting. But the hand!
The boy's first outcry was a rueful laugh,
As he swung toward them holding up the hand,   20
Half in appeal, but half as if to keep
The life from spilling. Then the boy saw all—
Since he was old enough to know, big boy
Doing a man's work, though a child at heart—
He saw all spoiled. "Don't let them cut my hand off—
The doctor, when he comes. Don't let him, sister!"
So. But the hand was gone already.
The doctor put him in the dark of ether.
He lay and puffed his lips out with his breath.
And then—the watcher at his pulse took fright.   30
No one believed. They listened at his heart.
Little—less—nothing!—and that ended it.
No more to build on there. And they, since they
Were not the one dead, turned to their affairs.

Robert Frost

Poetry is man's rebellion against being what he is.

James Branch Cabell

She Dwelt among the Untrodden Ways

She dwelt among the untrodden ways
  Beside the springs of Dove.
A Maid whom there were none to praise
  And very few to love;

A violet by a mossy stone
  Half hidden from the eye!
—Fair as a star, when only one
  Is shining in the sky.

She lived unknown, and few could know
  When Lucy ceased to be;
But she is in her grave, and, oh,
  The difference to me!

William Wordsworth

Ode on Solitude

Happy the man, whose wish and care
  A few paternal acres bound,
Content to breathe his native air,
    In his own ground.

Whose herds with milk, whose fields with bread,
  Whose flocks supply him with attire,
Whose trees in summer yield him shade,
    In winter fire.

Blest, who can unconcern'dly find,
  Hours, days and years slide soft away,
In health of body, peace of mind,
    Quiet by day,

Sound sleep by night; study and ease,
  Together mixt; sweet recreation;
And innocence which most does please,
    With meditation.

Thus let me live, unseen, unknown,
  Thus unlamented let me die,
Steal from the world, and not a stone
    Tell where I lie.

Alexander Pope

Song of the Horseman

Córdoba.
Remote and lonely.

Jet-black mare and full round moon,
With olives in my saddle bags,
Although I know the road so well
I shall not get to Córdoba.

Across the plain, across the wind,
Jet-black mare and full red moon,
Death is gazing down upon me,
Down from the towers of Córdoba.

Ay! The road so dark and long.
Ay! My mare so tired yet brave.
Death is waiting for me there
Before I get to Córdoba

Córdoba.
Remote and lonely.

Translated from the Spanish by Roy Campbell

F. Garcia Lorca

Crossing the Bar

Sunset and evening star,
    And one clear call for me!
And may there be no moaning of the bar,
    When I put out to sea,

But such a tide as moving seems asleep,
    Too full for sound and foam,
When that which drew from out the boundless deep
    Turns again home.

Twilight and evening bell,
    And after that the dark!
And may there be no sadness of farewell,
    When I embark;

For tho' from out our bourne of Time and Place
    The flood may bear me far,
I hope to see my Pilot face to face
    When I have crost the bar.

Alfred, Lord Tennyson

There are two ways of coming close to poetry. One is by writing poetry.
  But as I say, there is another way to come close to poetry, fortunately, and that is in the reading of it, not as linguistics, not as history, not as anything but poetry.

Robert Frost

What's Poetry Doing to Us!?

Dorothy Parker's poetry makes us bitter.
Paul Simon's poetry makes us mellow.

Amy Lowell's poetry paints a picture.
Irving Layton's poetry erases pictures.

Robert Frost's poetry talks to us.
Alden Nowlan's poetry chats with us.

Bobby Burns' poetry makes us fall in love.
John Betjeman's poetry makes us fall out of love.

William Carlos Williams' poetry humbles us.
e. e. cummings' poetry baffles us.

Ogden Nash's poetry makes us laugh.
Gwendolyn MacEwen's poetry makes us wonder.

Andrei Voznesensky's poetry makes us say "I've been there."
Eliot's poetry makes us want to get out of there.

Gerard Manley Hopkins' poetry makes us kneel.
Paul Hewson's poetry makes us get up and dance.

A. E. Housman's poetry makes us want to write.
Dylan Thomas' poetry makes us want to read.

D. H. Lawrence's poetry asks us to wake up.
William Wordsworth's poetry lulls us to sleep.

Yeats' poetry makes us purchase a dictionary.
Margaret Atwood's poetry makes us purchase a newspaper.

Theodore Roethke's poetry walks us outside in nature.
Raymond Souster's poetry takes us downtown.

And our own poetry tells us who we are, keeps us honest, real, sincere, and alive. And maybe even will set us free.

•• **A** poet sees spirit as well as fact.

F arewell

A little while
and
I will be gone from among you,
whither I cannot tell.
From nowhere we come;
into nowhere we go.

What is life?
It is a flash of a firefly
in the night.
It is a breath of a buffalo
in the winter time.
It is the little shadow
that runs across the grass
and loses itself in the sunset.

Isapo-muxika (Crowfoot)

A poet is somebody who feels, and who expresses his feeling through words.

This may sound easy. It isn't.

A lot of people think or believe or know they feel—but that's thinking or believing or knowing: not feeling. And poetry is feeling—not knowing or believing or thinking.

Almost anybody can learn to think or believe or know, but not a single human being can be taught to feel. Why? Because whenever you think or you believe or you know, you're a lot of other people: but the moment you feel, you're nobody-but-yourself.

e. e. cummings

• • • • •

Life is response to the world within and around us. Our responses are intellectual, emotional, behavioural, spiritual, physical. Pure experience is a transitory awareness. It is all here and then gone…. It lives only in our fading, evolving memory, unless we capture it in
- line and colour (the painter)
- melody and harmony (the musician)
- form and dimension (the sculptor)
- movement (the dancer)
- words (the poet).

Art solidifies experience.

Johnnie's Poem

Look! I've written a poem!
Johnnie says
and hands it to me
      and it's about
      his grandfather dying
      last summer, and me
      in the hospital
and I want to cry,
don't you see, because it doesn't matter
if it's not very good:
      what matters is he knows
and it was me, his father, who told him
      you write poems about what
      you feel deepest and hardest.

Alden Nowlan

• • A poem
a moment memoried,
a marriage of words
and space and spunk

Primer Lesson

Look out how you use proud words.
When you let proud words go, it is
    not easy to call them back.
They wear long boots, hard boots; they
    walk off proud; they can't hear you
    calling—
Look out how you use proud words.

Carl Sandburg

Phone Booth

Someone is loose in Moscow who won't stop
Ringing my phone.
Whoever-it-is listens, then hangs up.
Dial tone.

What do you want? A bushel of rhymes or so?
An autograph? A bone?
Hello?
Dial tone.

Someone's lucky number, for all I know,
Is the same, worse luck, as my own.
Hello!
Dial tone.

Or perhaps it's an angel calling collect
To invite me to God's throne.
Damn, I've been disconnected.
Dial tone.

Or is it my old conscience, my power of choice
To which I've grown
A stranger, and which no longer knows my voice?
Dial tone.

Are you standing there in some subway station, stiff
And hatless in the cold,
With your finger stuck in the dial as if
In a ring of gold?

And is there, outside the booth, a desperate throng
Tapping its coins on the glass, chafing its hands,
Like a line of people who have been waiting long
To be measured for wedding bands?

I hear you breathe and blow into some remote
Mouthpiece, and as you exhale
The lapels of my coat
Flutter like pennants in a gale.

The planet's communications are broken.
I'm tired of saying *hello*,
My questions might as well be unspoken.
Into the void my answers go.

Thrown together, together
With you, with you unknown.
Hello. Hello. Hello there.
Dial tone. Dial tone. Dial tone.

Translated from the Russian by Richard Wilbur

Andrei Voznesensky

•• **W**hat is a poem?

*Poetry is the shape and shade and size
of words as they hum, strum, jig and
gallop along.*

Dylan Thomas

Poetry is a kind of wild justice.

Susan Musgrave

*Poetry is a response to the daily
necessity of getting the world right.*

Wallace Stevens

Poetry is the algebra of the heart.

e. e. cummings

*Poetry is not a turning loose of emotion, but an escape
from emotion; it is not the expression of personality, but
an escape from personality. But, of course, only those
who have personality and emotions know what it means
to want to escape from these things.*

T. S. Eliot

*Has any poet or critic successfully defined poetry? They
talk about it in such very different terms that it is difficult to
believe that they are describing the same activity.*

Elizabeth Drew

•• A poem
a plea, a pester,
a please,
a package of words

> *A poem is a small machine made out of words.*
>
> **William Carlos Williams**

The Eagle

He clasps the crag with crooked hands;
Close to the sun in lonely lands,
Ringed with the azure world, he stands.

The wrinkled sea beneath him crawls;
He watches from his mountain walls,
And like a thunderbolt he falls.

Alfred, Lord Tennyson

We Real Cool

The Pool Players.
Seven at the Golden Shovel.

We real cool. We
Left school. We

Lurk late. We
Strike straight. We

Sing sin. We
Thin gin. We

Jazz June. We
Die soon.

Gwendolyn Brooks

Immigrant

the suffering mouth
twists with great effort
to correctly pronounce
the word
in a foreign
language.

Aldo Bruno

Nature

! ? —.

Fulvio Ciano

> There's poetry all over the place.
>
> **Robert Lowell**

The Donkey

When fishes flew and forests walked
    And figs grew upon thorn,
Some moment when the moon was blood
    Then surely I was born;

With monstrous head and sickening cry
    And ears like errant wings,
The devil's walking parody
    On all four-footed things.

The tattered outlaw of the earth,
    Of ancient crooked will;
Starve, scourge, deride me: I am dumb,
    I keep my secret still.

Fools! For I also had my hour;
    One far fierce hour and sweet:
There was a shout about my ears,
    And palms before my feet.

G. K. Chesterton

T
HEY
OOK
HE

O
HE
ABLE

HEN
HEY
RIED
O

RINK
  i

Gerry Gorman

Apparently with no surprise
To any happy Flower
The Frost beheads it at its play—
In accidental power—
The blonde Assassin passes on—
The Sun proceeds unmoved
To measure off another Day
For an Approving God.

Emily Dickinson

The Scot in a kilt
Must never tilt.

Ian Riswick

P oem for an Audience of One

Why do you write?
someone has asked me.
Is it for fame or fortune?
Do you wish to communicate
to a larger audience?
Have you an important message?

I would like to say,
though I don't,
that I write for none of these reasons.

I am writing now
to pass the time
while I am waiting
for you to telephone.

Elizabeth Brewster

S mall Blue Thing

Today I am
a small blue thing
Like a marble
or an eye

With my knees against my mouth
I am perfectly round
I am watching you

I am cold against your skin
You are perfectly reflected
I am lost inside your pocket   10
I am lost against
your fingers

I am falling down the stairs
I am skipping on the sidewalk
I am thrown against the sky
I am raining down in pieces
I am scattering like light
Scattering like light
Scattering like light

Today I am   20
a small blue thing
Made of china
made of glass

I am cool and smooth and curious
I never blink
I am turning in your hand
Turning in your hand

small blue thing

Suzanne Vega

A poet is someone who shares
thoughts,
   emotions,
   experiences
with others.

A poet is a worker in words.

She recreates the world in her own way through words.

A poet precisely pins his words on the page. He creatively arranges them in delightful and aesthetic patterns, both aural and visual.

A poet makes statements about the human condition and enlarges our capacity to see.

The Greeks called him a Poet, which name, hath as the most excellent, gone through other languages. It cometh of this word Poiein *which is, to make: wherein I know not whether by luck or wisdom, we Englishmen have met with the Greeks in calling him a maker....*

Poesy therefore is an art of imitation, for so Aristotle *termeth it in his word* Mimesis, *that is to say, a representing, counterfeiting, or figuring forth: to speak metaphorically, a speaking picture.*

Sir Philip Sidney
A Defence of Poetry *(1580)*

a poet = a maker
poetry = a speaking picture

• • • • •

Below are the last three stanzas of "Stopping by Woods on a Snowy Evening" in Robert Frost's handwriting.

The poem grew out of a real experience. He stopped in winter at night by a dark forest. He was driving a team of horses.

The famous seven words of the final two verses were intact from the moment of conception.

Stopping by Woods on a Snowy Evening

Whose woods these are I think I know.
His house is in the village though;
He will not see me stopping here
To watch his woods fill up with snow.

My little horse must think it queer
To stop without a farmhouse near
Between the woods and frozen lake
The darkest evening of the year.

He gives his harness bells a shake
To ask if there is some mistake.
The only other sound's the sweep
Of easy wind and downy flake.

The woods are lovely, dark and deep.
But I have promises to keep,
And miles to go before I sleep,
And miles to go before I sleep.

Robert Frost

How can I know what I think till I see what I say?

E.M. Forster

He [the poet] unlocks our chains and admits us to a new scene.

Ralph Waldo Emerson

Thoughts

When I can make my thoughts come forth
    To walk like ladies up and down,
Each one puts on before the glass
    Her most becoming hat and gown.

But oh, the shy and eager thoughts
    That hide and will not get them dressed,
Why is it that they always seem
    So much more lovely than the rest?

Sara Teasdale

Anatomy of Music

On three strings, the frogs
accompany the stars

D. G. Jones

The Hitch-hiker

E. J. Barry

It is tremendously important that great poetry be written, it makes no jot of difference who writes it.

Ezra Pound

turn stone into sunlight,
language into fire,
words into poems...

Art solidifies experience!

There is no secret to writing a poem.
People have a deep inner compulsion to make things of
beauty out of their experience. Take some words...create.
Create your own booklet of ten poems.

Take some words.
Arrange them on the page.
Paint a picture in words.
Make a speaking picture.

Make a poem.

For whatever embryo the poem starts from - an
event, an emotion, a character, a scene, an insight,
an idea - its theme never exists in isolation.

Elizabeth Drew

All there is to writing is having ideas. To learn to write
is to learn to have ideas.

Robert Frost

The writer wants his pen to turn stone into sunlight,
language into fire.

Bernard Malamud

Poetry is a picture-making factory.

1. **SIMILE:** A direct comparison between two unlike things introduced by *like* or *as.*

   "His *hands* were like *wild birds.*"
   John Updike

2. **METAPHOR:** A comparison between two unlike things.

   "An *agèd man* is but a paltry thing,
   A *tattered coat* upon a stick."
   William Butler Yeats

3. **PERSONIFICATION:** To give human characteristics to inanimate objects, animals, or abstract ideas.

   "*Time* let me play and be
   Golden in the *mercy of his means,*"
   Dylan Thomas

4. **HYPERBOLE:** Exaggeration.

   "And I will love thee still, my dear,
   Till *a' the seas gang dry.*"
   Robert Burns

5. **MOOD:** The emotional environment of the poem, also called *atmosphere.* "Farewell" has a quiet, reflective mood:

   "What is life
   It is a flash of a firefly . . . . "
   Isapo-muxika (Crowfoot)

6. **JUXTAPOSITION:** Two or more things are placed side by side, even though they usually aren't associated with each other.

   "Today I am
   a small blue thing
   Like a *marble*
   or an *eye*"
   Suzanne Vega

The Poet . . . he can make every word he speaks draw blood.

Walt Whitman

imagery · any strong sense presentation establishing "picture" (impression) ex)

74

Poems are meant to be heard.

1. **ALLITERATION:** The neighbouring words begin with the same letter or sound.

   "And wake to the farm forever fled"
   Dylan Thomas

2. **ASSONANCE:** Similarity of vowel sounds.

   "In silence deep the legions stream,"
   Herman Melville

3. **CONSONANCE:** Repetition of consonant sounds.

   "A springful of larks in a rolling/ Cloud"
   Dylan Thomas

4. **ONOMATOPOEIA:** The sound of the word mimics the sound to which it refers.

   buzz crackle blurt boom

5. **EUPHONY:** The inherent sweetness of the sound.

   chimes hush vermilion wisdom

6. **CACOPHONY:** The harsh, discordant sound.

   "Knock-kneed, coughing like hags, we cursed through sludge,"
   Wilfred Owen

7. **RHYME:** Similarity of sounds between words.

8. **RHYTHM:** The flow of the poem as created by alternating stressed and unstressed syllables.

The best words in their best order.

Samuel Taylor Coleridge

rhyme =similarity of sounds between words
=the glue that holds the poem together
=a musical device

Types of Rhyme

1. **SINGLE OR MASCULINE RHYME:** Similarity of sound in one syllable.

   "There was a young fellow named *Hall*,
   Who fell in the spring in the *fall*."

2. **FEMININE RHYME:** Two syllables rhyme.

   "A truth that's told with bad *intent*
   Beats all the lies you can *invent*."
   William Blake

3. **TRIPLE RHYME:** Three syllables similar in sound.

   vic*torious*
   gl*orious*

4. **EYE RHYME OR IMPERFECT RHYME:** The words rhyme to the eye but not the ear.

   have   stood   loves
   gave   blood   moves

5. **INTERNAL RHYME:** Rhymes within the verse itself rather than at the end of the line.

   "In mist or *cloud*, on mast or *shroud*,"
   Samuel Taylor Coleridge

It surely isn't a crime
To write a poem that doesn't rhyme.

Jan Krasnodebski

rhythm =the rise and fall of stress in a poetic line
=the flow of the words

/ = stressed syllable

∪ = unstressed syllable

Types of Rhythm

1. **IAMBIC** ∪ / : oppose, delight, amuse, eject
2. **ANAPESTIC** ∪∪ / : disappear, interrupt, undergo
3. **TROCHAIC** / ∪ : gather, heartless, feeling
4. **DACTYLIC** / ∪∪ : merrily, happiness, sentiment
5. **SPONDAIC** / / : humdrum, heartbreak, wineglass

- A *FOOT* is one of the five groupings of stressed and unstressed syllables shown above.
- *METRE* depends on the number of feet in a line.

MONOMETRE (1 foot) > silence

DIMETRE (2 feet) > In a land / far away

TRIMETRE (3 feet) > "Man and / boy stood / cheering / by"

TETRAMETRE (4 feet) > "Double, / double / toil and / trouble;"

PENTAMETRE (5 feet) > "When I / do count / the clock /
that tells / the time"

from **M**etrical Feet

Trochee trips from long to short;

From long to long in solemn sort
Slow Spondee stalks; strong foot! yet ill able
Ever to come up with Dactyl trisyllable.
Iambics march from short to long—
With a leap and a bound the swift Anapests throng; . . .

Samuel Taylor Coleridge

"Click."
I Hear and I Forget.
I See and I Remember.
I Do and I Understand.
"Click."

This unit is about writing poetry. When you understand what the poet is doing in a poem you get the "click," the artistic "click."

Coming to know someone else's poem is one way of coming to know your own potential poems.

"Click."

As the Chinese proverb says, "I Do and I Understand." The way to write a poem is just to do it. There is no special recipe to be followed. There is no mysterious potion you drink to write a poem.

Poems are made of words. The poet is a worker with words. The poet observes what is outside and what is inside. The poet hears the heartbeat of the universe, hears the silence of his or her own heart. The poet arranges words on a page.

"Click."

The words take a special shape. The words dance in the lines of the poem. The words stand up on their new legs and shout.

"Click."

Where does a poem start? With an image, a moment of insight, a symbol, a portrait, a conversation, a monologue, a joke, an imitation.

"Click."

Write a poem.

•• ## Create a picture in words

The Pond

Cold, wet leaves
Floating on moss-coloured water,
And the croaking of frogs—
Cracked bell-notes in the twilight.

Amy Lowell

Night

The dark steep roofs chisel
The infinity of the sky:

But the white moonlight gables
Resemble
Still hands at prayer.

Herbert Read

The Six-Quart Basket

The six-quart basket
one side gone
half the handle torn off

sits in the centre of the lawn
and slowly fills up
with the white fruits of the snow.

Raymond Souster

Fog

The fog comes
on little cat feet.

It sits looking
over harbour and city
on silent haunches
and then moves on.

Carl Sandburg

Young Woman at a Window

She sits with
tears on

her cheek
her cheek on

her hand
the child

in her lap
his nose

pressed
to the glass

William Carlos Williams

Wind and Silver

Greatly shining,
The Autumn moon floats in the thin sky;
And the fish-ponds shake their backs and
    flash their dragon scales
As she passes over them

Amy Lowell

A Year Passes

Beyond the porcelain fence of the pleasure garden,
I hear the frogs in the blue-green ricefields;
But the sword-shaped moon
Has cut my heart in two.

Amy Lowell

Night Clouds

The white mares of the moon rush along the sky
Beating their golden hoofs upon the glass Heavens;
The white mares of the moon are all standing on their hind legs
Pawing at the green porcelain doors of the remote Heavens.
Fly, Mares!
Strain your utmost,
Scatter the milky dust of stars,
Or the tiger sun will leap upon you and destroy you
With one lick of his vermilion tongue.

Amy Lowell

The Imagist Poem

Imagism = a name for a poetic form pioneered in the years 1907-1917 by a group of poets from England and America.

The Imagist poets placed stress on the precise, brittle beauty of the word or phrase. They presented their poems in concentrated, clear, exact, and colourful images.

Ezra Pound's imagist poem "In a Station of the Metro" was originally a 30-line poem.

In a Station of the Metro

The apparition of these faces in the crowd:
Petals on a wet, black bough.

Ezra Pound

Tenets of the Imagist Movement

1. Express the topic directly – either from the objective or subjective point of view.

2. Present the topic in images (word pictures). Use vivid, colourful images and not vague, cerebral generalities.

3. Employ the exact word, not the nearly exact word.

4. Write using the language of the senses. Appeal to colour, sound, taste, touch, smell.

5. Make the poem brief, economical, without any unnecessary words. Concentration is the essence of poetry.

6. Use free verse rhythms – cadence based on the natural rhythms of speech.

The poet becomes an expert packer of suitcases.

Sylvia Plath

I Wanted to Smash

I wanted to smash
something, anything against
their dull, stupid faces,

but then you reached down
with a certain smile,
put a flower in my hand.

Raymond Souster

Hymn

melancholy amber
trickling
down
my
soul

aroma
of burnt
honey
on an
autumn
afternoon

Tiffany Stone

Nantucket

Flowers through the window
lavender and yellow

changed by white curtains—
Smell of cleanliness—

Sunshine of late afternoon—
On the glass tray

a glass pitcher, the tumbler
turned down, by which

a key is lying—And the
immaculate white bed

William Carlos Williams

Church Bells, Montreal

Against the hard clean
ring of the bells

measure the quick
whispered tick of our lives!

Raymond Souster

•• **L**ess is more

The Red Wheelbarrow

so much depends
upon

a red wheel
barrow

glazed with rain
water

beside the white
chickens.

William Carlos Williams

I think it only damages a poem to have the poet try to explain it.

Michael Ondaatje

Symbol = Anything that signifies something else.

Symbolism = In literature, the use of objects or actions to suggest other objects or actions, or to suggest ideas or emotions.

natural symbol
dove = peace
island = isolation

conventional symbol
flag = patriotism
expensive car = wealth and status

private symbol
"lantern that wouldn't burn" = diminishing life-force
"pitch-dark limitless grove" = unknowable eternity
"someone he had to obey" = ??

The Draft Horse

With a lantern that wouldn't burn
In too frail a buggy we drove
Behind too heavy a horse
Through a pitch-dark limitless grove.

And a man came out of the trees
And took our horse by the head
And reaching back to his ribs
Deliberately stabbed him dead.

The ponderous beast went down
With a crack of a broken shaft.
And the night drew through the trees
In one long invidious draft.

The most unquestioning pair
That ever accepted fate
And the least disposed to ascribe
Any more than we had to hate,

We assumed that the man himself
Or someone he had to obey
Wanted us to get down
And walk the rest of the way.

Robert Frost

·· Saying one thing and meaning one thing more

The Sick Rose

O Rose, thou art sick!
The invisible worm,
That flies in the night,
In the howling storm,

Has found out thy bed
Of crimson joy;
And his dark secret love
Does thy life destroy.

William Blake

The Clod and the Pebble

"Love seeketh not itself to please,
Nor for itself hath any care,
But for another gives its ease,
And builds a Heaven in Hell's despair."

So sung a little Clod of Clay,
Trodden with the cattle's feet,
But a Pebble of the brook
Warbled out these metres meet:

"Love seeketh only Self to please,
To bind another to its delight,
Joys in another's loss of ease,
And builds a Hell in Heaven's despite."

William Blake

Image = a word-picture
= a crystallized sensory experience
= "what rough beast...slouches towards
Bethlehem to be born?"

Imagery = a poem's images considered as a whole
= a poem's second voice, elusive and true
= "the widening gyre...the blood-dimmed
tide...a shape with lion body and the head of
a man...a rocking cradle"

The Second Coming

Turning and turning in the widening gyre
The falcon cannot hear the falconer;
Things fall apart; the centre cannot hold;
Mere anarchy is loosed upon the world,
The blood-dimmed tide is loosed, and everywhere
The ceremony of innocence is drowned;
The best lack all conviction, while the worst
Are full of passionate intensity.

Surely some revelation is at hand;
Surely the Second Coming is at hand.   10
The Second Coming! Hardly are those words out
When a vast image out of *Spiritus Mundi*
Troubles my sight: somewhere in sands of the desert
A shape with lion body and the head of a man,
A gaze blank and pitiless as the sun,
Is moving its slow thighs, while all about it
Reel shadows of the indignant desert birds.
The darkness drops again; but now I know
That twenty centuries of stony sleep
Were vexed to nightmare by a rocking cradle,   20
And what rough beast, its hour come round at last,
Slouches towards Bethlehem to be born?

William Butler Yeats

S pring

To what purpose, April, do you return again?
Beauty is not enough.
You can no longer quiet me with the redness
Of little leaves opening stickily.
I know what I know.
The sun is hot on my neck as I observe
The spikes of the crocus.
The smell of the earth is good.
It is apparent that there is no death.
But what does that signify?
Not only under ground are the brains of men
Eaten by maggots.
Life in itself
Is nothing,
An empty cup, a flight of uncarpeted stairs.
It is not enough that yearly, down this hill,
April
Comes like an idiot, babbling and strewing flowers.

Edna St. Vincent Millay

After great pain, a formal feeling comes—
The Nerves sit ceremonious, like Tombs—
The stiff Heart questions was it He, that bore,
And Yesterday, or Centuries before?

The Feet, mechanical, go round—
Of Ground, or Air, or Ought—
A Wooden way
Regardless grown,
A Quartz contentment, like a stone—

This is the Hour of Lead—
Remembered, if outlived,
As Freezing Persons recollect the Snow—
First—Chill—then Stupor—then the letting go—

Emily Dickinson

•• Sketch a portrait in words

Portrait of a Girl with Comic Book

Thirteen's no age at all. Thirteen is nothing.
It is not wit, or powder on the face,
Or Wednesday matinee, or misses' clothing,
Or intellect, or grace.
Twelve has its tribal customs. But thirteen
Is neither boys in battered cars nor dolls.
Not *Sara Crewe* or movie magazine,
Or pennants on the walls.

Thirteen keeps diaries and tropical fish
(A month, at most); scorns jumpropes in the spring;
Could not, would fortune grant it, name its wish;
Wants nothing, everything;
Has secrets from itself, friends it despises;
Admits none of the terrors that it feels;
Owns a half a hundred masks but no disguises;
And walks upon its heels.

Thirteen's anomalous—not that, not this:
Not folded bud, or wave that laps a shore,
Or moth proverbial from the chrysalis.
Is the one age defeats the metaphor.
Is not a town, like childhood, strongly walled
But easily surrounded, in no city.
Nor, quitted once, can it be quite recalled—
Not even with pity.

Phyllis McGinley

Poetry is a verdict.

Leonard Cohen

The raw material of poetry is human experience: all poetry is made from that. Not only from rare and subtle and mysterious and spiritual and abstract and esoteric experiences, but from all and every form of human experience.

Elizabeth Drew

The Prodigal Son

The child who used to play see him now thin and bowed
The child who used to weep see now his burned-out eyes
The child who danced around see him running after a streetcar
The child who longed for the moon see him satisfied with a mouthful of bread
The wild and rebellious child, the child at the end of the town
In the remote streets
The child of adventures
Of the ice of the river
The child perched on fences
See him now in the narrow road of his daily routine   10
The child free and lightly clothed, see him now
Disguised as a bill-board, a sandwich-man
Dressed up in cardboard laws, a prisoner of petty taboos
Subdued and trussed, see him hunted in the name of justice
The child of lovely red blood and of good blood
See him now the ghost of a tragic opera

The prodigal son
The child prodigy, look at him now as a man
The man of 'time is money' and the man of *bel canto*
The man riveted to his work which is to rivet all day   20
The man of the Sunday afternoons in slippers
And the interminable bridge parties
The numberless man of the sports of the few men
And the man of the small bank account
To pay for the burial of a childhood that died
Towards its fifteenth year

Translated from the French by F. R. Scott

Gilles Hénault

Mr. Flood's Party

Old Eben Flood, climbing alone one night
Over the hill between the town below
And the forsaken upland hermitage
That held as much as he should ever know
On earth again of home, paused warily.
The road was his with not a native near;
And Eben, having leisure, said aloud,
For no man else in Tilbury Town to hear:

"Well, Mr. Flood, we have the harvest moon
Again, and we may not have many more;   10
The bird is on the wing, the poet says,
And you and I have said it here before.
Drink to the bird." He raised up to the light
The jug that he had gone so far to fill,
And answered huskily: "Well, Mr. Flood,
Since you propose it, I believe I will."

Alone, as if enduring to the end
A valiant armour or scarred hopes outworn,
He stood there in the middle of the road
Like Roland's ghost winding a silent horn.   20
Below him, in the town among the trees,
Where friends of other days had honoured him,
A phantom salutation of the dead
Rang thinly till old Eben's eyes were dim.

Then, as a mother lays her sleeping child
Down tenderly, fearing it may awake,
He set the jug down slowly at his feet
With trembling care, knowing that most things break;
And only when assured that on firm earth
It stood, as the uncertain lives of men   30
Assuredly did not, he paced away,
And with his hand extended paused again:

"Well, Mr. Flood, we have not met like this
In a long time; and many a change has come
To both of us, I fear, since last it was
We had a drop together. Welcome home!"
Convivially returning with himself,
Again he raised the jug up to the light;
And with an acquiescent quaver said:
"Well, Mr. Flood, if you insist, I might.   40

"Only a very little, Mr. Flood—
For auld lang syne. No more, sir; that will do."
So, for the time, apparently it did,
And Eben evidently thought so too;
For soon amid the silver loneliness
Of night he lifted up his voice and sang,
Secure, with only two moons listening,
Until the whole harmonious landscape range—

"For auld lang syne." The weary throat gave out,   50
The last word wavered, and the song was done.
He raised again the jug regretfully
And shook his head, and was again alone.
There was not much that was ahead of him,
And there was nothing in the town below—
Where strangers would have shut the many doors
That many friends had opened long ago.

Edwin Arlington Robinson

The Knitting Club

She perches,
budgie-like,
tries to ignore me.
She tells me
I don't know what pain is,
sees me
as a creature
wanting to destroy her
and her culture of crochet.
We're all the same   10
she tells us.
(teenagers, that is.)
It wasn't that way
when she was my age,
oh, no.
She wants me to learn to knit
instead of having friends, of course.
Her life is to please
everyone but herself.
I let her string her own yarns.   20

Stacy Kozakavich

"Is My Team Ploughing"

"Is my team ploughing,
    That I was used to drive
And hear the harness jingle
    When I was man alive?"

Aye, the horses trample,
    The harness jingles now;
No change though you lie under
    The land you used to plough.

"Is football playing
    Along the river shore,
With lads to chase the leather,
    Now I stand up no more?"

Aye, the ball is flying,
    The lads play heart and soul;
The goal stands up, the keeper
    Stands up to keep the goal.

"Is my girl happy,
    That I thought hard to leave,
And has she tired of weeping
    As she lies down at eve?"

Aye, she lies down lightly,
    She lies not down to weep:
Your girl is well contented.
    Be still, my lad, and sleep.

"Is my friend hearty,
    Now I am thin and pine;
And has he found to sleep in
    A better bed than mine?"

Aye, lad, I lie easy,
    I lie as lads would choose;
I cheer a dead man's sweetheart.
    Never ask me whose.

A. E. Housman

An Irish Airman Foresees His Death

I know that I shall meet my fate
Somewhere among the clouds above;
Those that I fight I do not hate,
Those that I guard I do not love;
My country is Kiltartan Cross,
My countrymen Kiltartan's poor,
No likely end could bring them loss
Or leave them happier than before.
Nor law, nor duty bade me fight,
Nor public men, nor cheering crowds,
A lonely impulse of delight
Drove to this tumult in the clouds;
I balanced all, brought all to mind,
The years to come seemed waste of breath,
A waste of breath the years behind
In balance with this life, this death.

William Butler Yeats

Grandmother in White

No, I don't want to sit still in my sweater
but with all these sheets I feel snowed in.

Besides, where could I go tonight? The halls are
all closed. I'll leave the light off—the way

it glares when I already am blind enough.
My nurse on her rounds looks in, looking

so much like the moon that I know she's smiling
but otherwise I am quite alone

and quite at a loss. I keep dreaming
up flowers though I've got no crepe or tissue

papers to make them come true and my fingers
feel boney, the skin worn through, useless

unless I can peel it back into
petals and become my own best handicraft.

Yes, my hands cupped together on the bedclothes
have already gone half numb and pale

as frost before dawn. Before long my nurse will
come by and see an Arctic blue rose.

Daniel David Moses

93

My Last Duchess
Ferrara

That's my last Duchess painted on the wall,
Looking as if she were alive. I call
That piece a wonder, now: Frà Pandolf's hands
Worked busily a day, and there she stands.
Will 't please you sit and look at her? I said
"Frà Pandolf" by design, for never read
Strangers like you that pictured countenance,
The depth and passion of its earnest glance,
But to myself they turned (since none puts by
The curtain I have drawn for you, but I)   10
And seemed as they would ask me, if they durst,
How such a glance came there; so, not the first
Are you to turn and ask thus. Sir, 'twas not
Her husband's presence only, called that spot
Of joy into the Duchess' cheek: perhaps
Frà Pandolf chanced to say, "Her mantle laps
Over my lady's wrist too much," or "Paint
Must never hope to reproduce the faint
Half-flush that dies along her throat:" such stuff
Was courtesy, she thought, and cause enough   20
For calling up that spot of joy. She had
A heart—how shall I say?—too soon made glad,
Too easily impressed; she liked whate'er
She looked on, and her looks went everywhere.
Sir, 'twas all one! My favour at her breast,
The dropping of the daylight in the West,
The bough of cherries some officious fool
Broke in the orchard for her, the white mule
She rode with round the terrace—all and each
Would draw from her alike the approving speech,   30
Or blush, at least. She thanked men,—good! but thanked
Somehow—I know not how—as if she ranked
My gift of a nine-hundred-years-old name
With anybody's gift. Who'd stoop to blame
This sort of trifling? Even had you skill
In speech—(which I have not)—to make your will
Quite clear to such an one, and say, "Just this
Or that in you disgusts me; here you miss,
Or there exceed the mark"—and if she let
Herself be lessoned so, nor plainly set   40
Her wits to yours, forsooth, and made excuse,

—E'en then would be some stooping; and I choose
Never to stoop. Oh sir, she smiled, no doubt,
Whene'er I passed her; but who passed without
Much the same smile? This grew; I gave commands;
Then all smiles stopped together. There she stands
As if alive. Will 't please you rise? We'll meet
The company below, then. I repeat,
The Count your master's known munificence
Is ample warrant that no just pretence   50
Of mine for dowry will be disallowed;
Though his fair daughter's self, as I avowed
At starting, is my object. Nay, we'll go
Together down, sir. Notice Neptune, though,
Taming a sea-horse, thought a rarity,
Which Claus of Innsbruck cast in bronze for me!

Robert Browning

The dramatic monologue—a kind of poetry perfected by Robert Browning.

• the poet creates a character and a dramatic situation
• the poem is the character's monologue, spoken to another character who does not appear in the poem directly
• the dramatic monologue is a tour de force of theatre, of characterization

•• Write a poem on the lighter side

One Perfect Rose

A single flow'r he sent me, since we met.
    All tenderly his messenger he chose;
Deep-hearted, pure, with scented dew still wet—
    One perfect rose.

I knew the language of the floweret;
    "My fragile leaves," it said, "his heart enclose."
Love long has taken for his amulet
    One perfect rose.

Why is it no one ever sent me yet
    One perfect limousine, do you suppose?
Ah no, it's always just my luck to get
    One perfect rose.

Dorothy Parker

Bendix

This porthole overlooks a sea
Forever falling from the sky,
The water inextricably
Involved with buttons, suds, and dye.

Like bits of shrapnel, shards of foam
Fly heavenward; a bedsheet heaves,
A stocking wrestles with a comb,
And cotton angels wave their sleeves.

The boiling purgatorial tide
Revolves our dreary shorts and slips,
While Mother coolly bakes beside
Her little jugged apocalypse.

John Updike

nobody loses all the time

nobody loses all the time

i had an uncle named
Sol who was a born failure and
nearly everybody said he should have gone
into vaudeville perhaps because my Uncle Sol could
sing McCann He Was A Diver on Xmas Eve like Hell itself which
may or may not account for the fact that my Uncle

Sol indulged in that possibly most inexcusable
of all to use a highfalootin phrase
luxuries that is or to   10
wit farming and be
it needlessly
added

my Uncle Sol's farm
failed because the chickens
ate the vegetables so
my Uncle Sol had a
chicken farm till the
skunks ate the chickens when

my Uncle Sol   20
had a skunk farm but
the skunks caught cold and
died and so
my Uncle Sol imitated the
skunks in a subtle manner

or by drowning himself in the watertank
but somebody who'd given my Uncle Sol a Victor
Victrola and records while he lived presented to
him upon the auspicious occasion of his decease a
scrumptious not to mention splendiferous funeral with   30
tall boys in back gloves and flowers and everything and

i remember we all cried like the Missouri
when my Uncle Sol's coffin lurched because
somebody pressed a button
(and down went
my Uncle
Sol

and started a worm farm)

e. e. cummings

The Turtle

The turtle lives 'twixt plated decks.
Which practically conceal its sex.
I think it clever of the turtle
In such a fix to be so fertile.

Ogden Nash

Lather as You Go

Beneath this slab
John Brown is stowed.
He watched the ads,
And not the road.

Ogden Nash

In Divés' Dive

It is late at night and still I am losing,
But still I am steady and unaccusing.

As long as the Declaration guards
My right to be equal in number of cards,

It is nothing to me who runs the Dive.
Let's have a look at another five.

Robert Frost

Résumé

Razors pain you;
Rivers are damp;
Acids stain you;
And drugs cause cramp.
Guns aren't lawful;
Nooses give;
Gas smells awful;
You might as well live.

Dorothy Parker

Triolet against Sisters

Sisters are always drying their hair.
　　Locked into rooms, alone,
They pose at the mirror, shoulders bare,
Trying this way and that their hair,
Or fly importunate down the stair
　　to answer a telephone.
Sisters are always drying their hair,
　　Locked into rooms, alone.

Phyllis McGinley

Meditatio

When I carefully consider the curious habits of dogs
I am compelled to conclude
That man is the superior animal.

When I consider the curious habits of man
I confess, my friend, I am puzzled.

Ezra Pound

World's Shortest Pessimistic Poem

Hope?
Nope.

Robert Zend

A Chain of Haik

Japanese people
think it is quite boring to
finish their senten

I agree with them
we can guess anyway what
should come after the

We go to bed when
we are sleepy and not when
we finished what we

We die the same way
there are many unfinished
things to do when sud

Western reader, I
hope you will understand me,
and if not, you can

Robert Zend

A Subaltern's Love-Song

Miss J. Hunter Dunn, Miss J. Hunter Dunn,
Furnish'd and burnish'd by Aldershot sun,
What strenuous singles we played after tea,
We in the tournament—you against me!

Love-thirty, love-forty, oh! weakness of joy,
The speed of a swallow, the grace of a boy,
With carefullest carelessness, gaily you won,
I am weak from your loveliness, Joan Hunter Dunn.

Miss Joan Hunter Dunn, Miss Joan Hunter Dunn,
How mad I am, sad I am, glad that you won: 10
The warm-handled racket is back in its press,
But my shock-headed victor, she loves me no less.

Her father's euonymus shines as we walk,
And swing past the summer-house, buried in talk,
And cool the verandah that welcomes us in
To the six-o'clock news and a lime-juice and gin.

The scent of the conifers, sound of the bath,
The view from my bedroom of moss-dappled path,
As I struggle with double-end evening tie,
For we dance at the Golf Club, my victor and I.   20

On the floor of her bedroom lie blazer and shorts
And the cream-coloured walls are be-trophied with sports,
And westering, questioning settles the sun
On your low-leaded window, Miss Joan Hunter Dunn.

The Hillman is waiting, the light's in the hall,
The pictures of Egypt are bright on the wall,
My sweet, I am standing beside the oak stair
And there on the landing's the light on your hair.

By roads 'not adopted,' by woodlanded ways,
She drove to the club in the late summer haze,   30
Into nine-o'clock Camberley, heavy with bells
And mushroomy, pine-woody, evergreen smells.

Miss Joan Hunter Dunn, Miss Joan Hunter Dunn,
I can hear from the car-park the dance has begun.
Oh! full Surrey twilight! importunate band!
Oh! strongly adorable tennis-girl's hand!

Around us are Rovers and Austins afar,
Above us, the intimate roof of the car,
And here on my right is the girl of my choice,
With the tilt of her nose and the chime of her voice.   40

And the scent of her wrap, and the words never said,
And the ominous, ominous dancing ahead.
We sat in the car park till twenty to one
And now I'm engaged to Miss Joan Hunter Dunn.

John Betjeman

40 —— Love

middle	aged
couple	playing
ten	nis
when	the
game	ends
and	they
go	home
the	net
will	still
be	be
tween	them

Roger McGough

•• **I**mitate a serious piece of writing

Trees

I think that I shall never see
A poem lovely as a tree.

A tree whose hungry mouth is pressed
Against the earth's sweet flowing breast;

A tree that looks to God all day,
And lifts her leafy arms to pray;

A tree that may in summer wear
A nest of robins in her hair;

Upon whose bosom snow has lain;
Who intimately lives with rain.

Poems are made by fools like me,
But only God can make a tree.

Joyce Kilmer

Song of the Open Road
(after Joyce Kilmer)

I think that I shall never see
A billboard lovely as a tree.
Indeed, unless the billboards fall,
I'll never see a tree at all.

Ogden Nash

Mirror

When you look
into a mirror
it is not
yourself you see,
but a kind
of apish error
posed in fearful
symmetry.

John Updike

Parody: after Updike

LOOKING GNIKOOL
THROUGH HGUORHT
THE EHT
GLASS SSALG
I I
SEE EES
ME WE

Peter Barrett

from **H**amlet

Hamlet. "By and by" is easily said. Leave me, friends.

[*Exeunt all but Hamlet.*]

'Tis now the very witching time of night,
When churchyards yawn, and hell itself breathes out
Contagion to this world. Now could I drink hot blood
And do such bitter business as the day
Would quake to look on. Soft, now to my mother.
O heart, lose not thy nature; let not ever
The soul of Nero enter this firm bosom.
Let me be cruel, not unnatural;
I will speak daggers to her, but use none.
My tongue and soul in this be hypocrites:
How in my words somever she be shent,
To give them seals never, my soul, consent!

William Shakespeare

Parody: after Shakespeare

"Study and study" is easily said. Believe me, friends.
'Tis now the very cramming time of night,
When students yawn and fear itself comes out,
Contagion to this world. Now could I drink hot coffee,
As I do this bitter business the night
Would quake to look on. Exams! Now to my books.
O brain lose not thy knowledge, let not ever
The role of zero enter this term.
Let me do better, not as usual.
I will make cheatsheets, but use none
My mind and pen in this be hypocrites,
How in the world can this ever be learnt,
To study in advance never, my cerebrum, consent!

Dave Turner

GENRE = a certain kind of literature or poetry.

... the style of a poem and the poem itself are one.
Wallace Stevens

quatrain
ballad
sonnet
free verse
lyric poetry
haiku
limerick
epigram
shape poetry
cummingese
concrete poetry
computer poetry
corporate computer poetry

... a formally airtight compartment of words.
Dylan Thomas

A stanza = a unit of a poem
  = a grouping of two or more lines of poetry

Many poems are made up of several stanzas that have the same number of lines and pattern of rhyme and rhythm. A *couplet* is a stanza consisting of a pair of rhymed lines. A three-line stanza is called a *tercet*. The most common stanza is the *quatrain*—a four-line stanza.

Here are some typical rhyme schemes:

a	a	a	a
b	b	a	b
a	c	b	b
b	b	b	a

from In Memoriam (CVI)

Ring out the old, ring in the new,	a
Ring, happy bells, across the snow:	b
The year is going, let him go;	b
Ring out the false, ring in the true.	a

Alfred, Lord Tennyson

The Difference

'Twixt optimist and pessimist
  The difference is droll:
The optimist sees the doughnut;
  The pessimist sees the hole.

Anonymous

"Faith" is a fine invention
When Gentlemen can *see*—
But *Microscopes* are prudent
In an Emergency.

Emily Dickinson

Outwitted

He drew a circle that shut me out—
Heretic, rebel, a thing to flout.
But Love and I had the wit to win:
We drew a circle that took him in!

Edwin Markham

folk ballad = a story expressed through song
= a haunting, dramatic tale handed down from generation to generation

literary ballad = a narrative poem written in the ballad form
= a carefully crafted poem disguised as folk poetry

Ballads often are written in quatrains.

Many contemporary folk, country, and rock songs are ballads.

The Twa Corbies

As I was walking all alane,
I heard twa corbies making a mane,
The tane unto the t'other say,
"Where sall we gang and dine today?"

"In behint yon auld fail dyke,
I wot there lies a new-slain knight;
And naebody kens that he lies there,
But his hawk, his hound, and lady fair.

"His hound is to the hunting gane,
His hawk to fetch the wild-fowl hame,
His lady's ta'en another mate,
So we may mak our dinner sweet.

"Ye'll sit on his white hause-bane,
And I'll pike out his bonny blue een',
With ae lock o his gowden hair
We'll theek our nest when it grows bare.

"Mony a one for him makes mane,
But nane sall ken where he is gane;
O'er his white banes, when they are bare,
The wind sall blaw for evermair."

Anonymous

Fair Helen

I wish I were where Helen lies;
Night and day on me she cries;
O that I were where Helen lies
    On fair Kirconnell lea!

Curst be the heart that thought the thought,
And curst the hand that fired the shot,
When in my arms burd Helen dropt,
    And died to succour me!

O think na but my heart was sair
When my Love dropt down and spak nae mair!
I laid her down wi' meikle care
    On fair Kirconnell lea.

As I went down the water-side,
None but my foe to be my guide,
None but my foe to be my guide,
    On fair Kirconnell lea;

I lighted down my sword to draw,
I hackèd him in pieces sma',
I hackèd him in pieces sma',
    For her sake that died for me.

O Helen fair, beyond compare!
I'll make a garland of thy hair
Shall bind my heart for evermair
    Until the day I die.

O that I were where Helen lies!
Night and day on me she cries;
Out of my bed she bids me rise,
    Says, "Haste and come to me!"

O Helen fair! O Helen chaste!
If I were with thee, I were blest,
Where thou lies low and takes thy rest
    On fair Kirconnell lea.

I wish my grave were growing green,
A winding-sheet drawn ower my een,
And I in Helen's arms lying,
    On fair Kirconnell lea.

I wish I were where Helen lies;
Night and day on me she cries;
And I am weary of the skies,
    Since my Love died for me.

Anonymous

Ballad

O what is that sound which so thrills the ear
    Down in the valley drumming, drumming?
Only the scarlet soldiers, dear,
    The soldiers coming.

O what is that light I see flashing so clear
    Over the distance brightly, brightly?
Only the sun on their weapons, dear,
    As they step lightly.

O what are they doing with all that gear;
    What are they doing this morning, this morning?
Only the usual manoeuvres, dear,
    Or perhaps a warning.

O why have they left the road down there;
    Why are they suddenly wheeling, wheeling?
Perhaps a change in the orders, dear;
    Why are you kneeling?

O haven't they stopped for the doctor's care;
    Haven't they reined their horses, their horses?
Why, they are none of them wounded, dear,
    None of these forces.

O is it the parson they want, with white hair;
    Is it the parson, is it, is it?
No, they are passing his gateway, dear,
    Without a visit.

O it must be the farmer who lives so near,
    It must be the farmer, so cunning, cunning;
They have passed the farm already, dear,
    And now they are running.

O where are you going? Stay with me here.
    Were the vows you swore me deceiving, deceiving?
No, I promised to love you, dear,
    But I must be leaving.

O it's broken the lock and splintered the door,
    O it's the gate where they're turning, turning;
Their feet are heavy on the floor
    And their eyes are burning.

W. H. Auden

Wreck on the Highway

Last night I was out driving
Coming home at the end of the working day
I was riding alone through the drizzling rain
On a deserted stretch of a county two-lane
When I came upon a wreck on the highway

There was blood and glass all over
And there was nobody there but me
As the rain tumbled down hard and cold
I seen a young man lying by the side of the road
He cried Mister, won't you help me please

An ambulance finally came and took him to
     Riverside
I watched as they drove him away
And I thought of a girlfriend or a young wife
And a state trooper knocking in the middle of
     the night
To say your baby died in a wreck on the
     highway

Sometimes I sit up in the darkness
And I watch my baby as she sleeps
Then I climb in bed and hold her tight
I just lay there awake in the middle of the night
Thinking 'bout the wreck on the highway

Bruce Springsteen

The only cause for pessimism would be if
men and women ceased to write poetry,
and they don't.

Elizabeth Drew

Sadie and Maud

Maud went to college.
Sadie stayed at home.
Sadie scraped life
With a fine-tooth comb.

She didn't leave a tangle in.
Her comb found every strand
Sadie was one of the livingest chits
In all the land.

Sadie bore two babies
Under her maiden name.
Maud and Ma and Papa
Nearly died of shame.

When Sadie said her last so-long
Her girls struck out from home.
(Sadie had left as heritage
Her fine-tooth comb.)

Maud, who went to college,
Is a thin brown mouse.
She is living all alone
In this old house.

Gwendolyn Brooks

Holy Sonnet 10

Death, be not proud, though some have callèd thee
Mighty and dreadful, for thou art not so;
For those whom thou think'st thou dost overthrow
Die not, poor Death, nor yet canst thou kill me.
From rest and sleep, which but thy pictures be,
Much pleasure; then from thee much more must flow,
And soonest our best men with thee do go,
Rest of their bones, and soul's delivery.
Thou art slave to fate, chance, kings, and desperate men,
And dost with poison, war, and sickness dwell,
And poppy or charms can make us sleep as well
And better than thy stroke; why swell'st thou then?
One short sleep past, we wake eternally
And death shall be no more; Death, thou shalt die.

John Donne

Fast Run in the Junkyard

That junkyard fell down the side of the hill
like a river: baby buggy, black leather
cracked car back seat, sofa wind-siphoned
by a clutch of tangled wire hangers hanging on
like spiders. We stood and fell as momentum told us
toward somebody's sodden Sealey dying of galloping miasma,
jumped on bedsprings sprung to pogos, and leaped
for king-of-the-mountain where boxes and cans fountained
up the hill's other side. Sailing saucers, we rode
back down, flinging hat racks, burlap sacks, chairs cropped
of backs and flotsam crockery, breezed in league boots
back out of everybody's past hazards, up to the road
to break tar bubbles all-the-way-home where things
were wearing out as fast as we were growing up.

Jeannette Nichols

The Knockout

The bell clanged "Time!" again. The boxers sparred,
Creep-footed, tiger-muscled, cautious-eyed,
Love the bright pugilist with his glance enskied,
Fate swart as rock, indomitably hard.
Slashing the battle joined of bull and pard
With blows like hammerstrokes. A thick sob died
In the crowd's throat. Fate's poison-smile grew wide,
His mountainous fist ripped Love's too-careless guard.

Fate smashed the reeling struggle to the ropes,
Poised for the knockout; hurled his brute attack,
—And suddenly was lying on his back—
"Nine—Ten!" the slow words came like punctured hopes—
Laughing I clapped, and winked at languid Love.
I *knew* he had a star inside his glove!

Stephen Vincent Benét

Sonnet 116

Let me not to the marriage of true minds
Admit impediments. Love is not love
Which alters when it alteration finds,
Or bends with the remover to remove:
O, no! it is an ever-fixèd mark,
That looks on tempests and is never shaken;
It is the star to every wand'ring bark,
Whose worth's unknown, although his height be taken.
Love's not Time's fool, though rosy lips and cheeks
Within his bending sickle's compass come;
Love alters not with his brief hours and weeks,
But bears it out even to the edge of doom:—
  If this be error and upon me proved,
  I never writ, nor no man ever loved.

William Shakespeare

• • • • •

A sonnet = a 14-line poem
= iambic pentametre rhythm
= intricate rhyme scheme

1. **Petrarchan sonnet:** $\dfrac{8}{6} = \dfrac{\text{octave}}{\text{sestet}}$

2. **Shakespearean sonnet:** $\dfrac{12}{2} = \dfrac{\text{3 quatrains}}{\text{rhyming couplet}}$

3. **Curtal sonnet:** $\dfrac{6}{4.5} =$ a shortened sonnet developed by Hopkins

4. **Avant-garde sonnet . . .**

Aeronaut to His Lady

I
   Through
   Blue
Sky
Fly
   To
   You.
Why?

Sweet
     Love,
Feet
   Move
      So
      Slow!

Frank Sidgwick

Pied Beauty

Glory be to God for dappled things—
   For skies of couple-colour as a brinded cow;
     For rose-moles all in stipple upon trout that swim;
Fresh-firecoal chestnut-falls; finches' wings,
   Landscape plotted and pieced—fold, fallow, and plough;
     And all trades, their gear and tackle and trim.

All things counter, original, spare, strange;
   Whatever is fickle, freckled (who knows how?)
     With swift, slow; sweet, sour; adazzle, dim;
He fathers-forth whose beauty is past change:
       Praise him.

Gerard Manley Hopkins

•• The sonnet form is a special challenge to the artistry of the poet...

First Fight. Then Fiddle.

First fight. Then fiddle. Ply the slipping string
With feathery sorcery; muzzle the note
With hurting love; the music that they wrote
Bewitch, bewilder. Qualify to sing
Threadwise. Devise no salt, no hempen thing
For the dear instrument to bear. Devote
The bow to silks and honey. Be remote
A while from malice and from murdering.
But first to arms, to armour. Carry hate
In front of you and harmony behind.
Be deaf to music and to beauty blind.
Win war. Rise bloody, maybe not too late
For having first to civilize a space
Wherein to play your violin with grace

Gwendolyn Brooks

Tennis

Service is joy, to see or swing. Allow
All tumult to subside. Then tensest winds
Buffet, brace, viol and sweeping bow.
Courts are for love and volley. No one minds
The cruel ellipse of service and return,
Dancing white galliardes at tape or net
Till point, on the wire's tip, or the long burn-
ing arc to nethercourt marks game and set.
Purpose apart, perched like an umpire, dozes,
Dreams golden balls whirring through indigo.
Clay blurs the whitewash but day still encloses
The albinos, bonded in their flick and flow.
Playing in musicked gravity, the pair
Score liquid Euclids in foolscaps of air.

Margaret Avison

- short lines
- controlled but irregular rhythm
- fixed rhyme scheme given up in favour of other kinds of wordplay
- contemporary poetry is often written in free verse

The Islands

There are two of them:

One larger, with steep granite
cliffs facing us, dropping sheer
to the deep lake;

the other smaller, closer
to land, with a reef running
out from it and dead trees
grey, waist-high in the water.

We know they are alone
and always will be.   10

The lake takes care of that
and if it went,
they would be hills
and still demand
separateness
from the eye.

Yet, standing on the cliff
(the two
of us)
on our bigger island,   20
looking,

we find it pleasing
(it soothes our instinct for
symmetry, proportion,
for company perhaps)

that there are two of them.

Margaret Atwood

A shadow of ourselves…
- subjective
- personal
- emotional

Graduation

Shuffling down the empty halls
I watch the shadows run and hide.
The silence calls for me to leave,
But another voice speaks to me
          from the past:

I sweep the leaves which fall
          from summer boughs
I pile them high and light a match
          and watch
the creeping flames devour them one
          by one
and in a moment, flames with hungry lust
burn in scarlet fury and turn to ash
and in a silver plume of smoke
the silence calls for me to leave.

Mike Lewandowski

When I am dead, my dearest,
     Sing no sad songs for me;
Plant thou no roses at my head,
     Nor shady cypress tree:
Be the green grass above me
     With showers and dewdrops wet:
And if thou wilt, remember,
     And if thou wilt, forget.

I shall not see the shadows,
     I shall not feel the rain;
I shall not hear the nightingale
     Sing on as if in pain:
And dreaming through the twilight
     That doth not rise nor set,
Haply I may remember,
     And haply may forget.

Christina Rossetti

Where Have You Gone

Where have you gone

with your confident
walk with
your crooked smile

why did you leave
me
when you took your
laughter
and departed

are you aware that
with you
went the sun
all light
and what few stars
there were?

where have you gone
with your confident
walk your
crooked smile the
rent money
in one pocket and
my heart
in another…

Mari Evans

Annabel Lee

It was many and many a year ago,
    In a kingdom by the sea,
That a maiden there lived whom you may know
    By the name of Annabel Lee;—
And this maiden she lived with no other thought
    Than to love and be loved by me.

I was a child and *she* was a child,
    In this kingdom by the sea,
But we loved with a love that was more than love—
    I and my Annabel Lee—   10
With a love that the wingèd seraphs in Heaven
    Coveted her and me.

And this was the reason that, long ago,
    In this kingdom by the sea,
A wind blew out of a cloud, chilling
    My beautiful Annabel Lee;
So that her high-born kinsmen came
    And bore her away from me,
To shut her up in a sepulchre
    In this kingdom by the sea.   20

The angels, not half so happy in Heaven,
    Went envying her and me:—
Yes!—that was the reason (as all men know,
    In this kingdom by the sea)
That the wind came out of the cloud, by night,
    Chilling and killing my Annabel Lee.

But our love it was stronger by far than the love
    Of those who were older than we—
    Of many far wiser than we—
And neither the angels in Heaven above,   30
    Nor the demons down under the sea,
Can ever dissever my soul from the soul
    Of the beautiful Annabel Lee:—

For the moon never beams without bringing me dreams
    Of the beautiful Annabel Lee;
And the stars never rise but I feel the bright eyes
    Of the beautiful Annabel Lee;
And so, all the night-tide, I lie down by the side
Of my darling,—my darling,—my life and my bride,
    In her sepulchre there by the sea—   40
    In her tomb by the sounding sea.

Edgar Allan Poe

Pippa's Song

The year's at the spring,
And day's at the morn;
Morning's at seven;
The hill-side's dew-pearl'd;
The lark's on the wing;
The snail's on the thorn;
God's in His heaven—
All's right with the world!

Robert Browning

The Bird

The bird you captured is dead.
I told you it would die
but you would not learn
from my telling. You wanted
to cage a bird in your hands
and learn to fly.

Listen again.
You must not handle birds.
They cannot fly through your fingers.
You are not a nest
and a feather is
not made of blood and bone.

Only words
can fly for you like birds
on the wall of the sun.
A bird is a poem
that talks of the end of cages.

Patrick Lane

The Look

Strephon kissed me in the spring,
    Robin in the fall,
But Colin only looked at me
    And never kissed at all.

Strephon's kiss was lost in jest,
    Robin's lost in play,
But the kiss in Colin's eyes
    Haunts me night and day.

Sara Teasdale

The Clearing

Growing old is a withdrawing
    From the fire
In the little clearing
    Of desire.

It is moving to cooler
    Air on the fringe
Where trees are nearer
    And voices strange.

We need not shudder
    Or be afraid
Till we cross the border
    Of that dark wood.

Till in the dark glow
    Suddenly
We find the shadow
    Become the tree.

F. R. Scott

- One of the shortest verse forms.
- The traditional Japanese haiku has seventeen syllables in three lines.

With a crunching sound	5
the praying mantis devours	7
the face of a bee.	5

Yamaguchi Seichi

- Seventeen syllables equals one exhalation of breath, one flowing-out of the soul.
- Contemporary haiku often deviate from the traditional pattern, but the brevity and intensity are always preserved.

Shadows

in the setting sun
the players' shadows converse
on a frozen pond.

Dave Turner

black roses burning
in a bright blue room—my thoughts
explode in white.

Greg Guest

Polar Bear and Rifle

on the tundra bleak
a white king falls! BLOODY DEED —
THE RIFLEMAN BLINKS.

Peter Knopfel

> haiku = one intense moment of awareness
> = a still-life painting or photograph
> = "simply what is happening at this moment in this place" *Basho*
> = a mood, an atmosphere, one simple observation

Wolfe Lake Sunset

The glass is bleeding
From a deep western wound
Only the loon can heal.

Fred Sengmueller

Suicide's Note

The calm,
Cool face of the river
Asked me for a kiss.

Langston Hughes

After a heated argument
I go out to the street
and become a motorcycle.

Kaneko Tōta

Bicycle Race

Twenty moving pastels
Smeared across
A page of asphalt.

Gregory Dimmock

The Sudden Chillness

The piercing chill I feel:
my dead wife's comb, in our bedroom,
under my heel....

Buson

Haiku

I light my cigar
on a tree's lee side
while a dog waits politely.

Milton Acorn

Limericks are the clowns of the poetic community.

They are difficult to write because they have a set form. They always rhyme aabba, and they have an anapestic rhythm. Lines one, two, and five have three feet; lines three and four have two feet.

There was/an old man/from Nantucket   a

Who kept/all his cash/in a bucket   a

But his daugh/ter named Nan   b

Ran away/with a man   b

And as/for the bucket, Nantucket   a

Anonymous

There was a young fellow named Hall,
Who fell in the spring in the fall.
    'Twould have been a sad thing
    If he'd died in the spring,
But he didn't—he died in the fall.

Anonymous

Absurd Limerick

There was a young man from Perth
Who was born on the day of his birth.
    He was wed, so they say
    On his wife's wedding day
And he died on his last day on earth.

John Robert Colombo

A diner while dining at Crewe
Found quite a large mouse in his stew.
    Said the waiter, "Don't shout
    And wave it about,
Or the rest will be wanting one, too."

Anonymous

There was a young fellow named Fisher,
Who was fishing for fish in a fissure,
    When a cod with a grin
    Pulled the fisherman in.
Now they're fishing the fissure for Fisher.

Anonymous

epigram =a rhyming couplet
=a compact, jewel-hard comment
=short-order poetry

from **A**uguries of Innocence

A truth that's told with bad intent
Beats all the lies you can invent.

William Blake

I am his highness' dog at Kew.
Pray tell me, sir, whose dog are you?

Alexander Pope

Fatigue

I'm tired of Love: I'm still more tired of Rhyme.
But Money gives me pleasure all the time.

Hilaire Belloc

The Philosopher

I?
Why?

Anonymous

East and West

In this country I speak freely, without fear;
but no one in this lethargy will ever hear.

Back *there*, all listen to what I have to say;
especially the secret police, who lead me away.

Translated from the Hungarian by Eric Johnson

George Faludy

epigram (n)—a short, crisp sharp saying in prose or verse, frequently characterized by acidity and acerbity and sometimes by wisdom.

Ambrose Bierce

The poet manipulates letters, words, and lines to create a poem with a distinct shape. The shape of the poem suggests the poem's topic.

George Herbert (1593-1633) wrote this type of verse in the 17th century.

The Altar

A broken ALTAR, Lord, thy servant reares,
Made of a heart, and cemented with teares:
  Whose parts are as thy hand did frame;
  No workman's tool hath touch'd the same.
        A HEART alone
        Is such a stone,
        As nothing but
        Thy pow'r doth cut.
        Wherefore each part
        Of my hard heart
        Meets in this frame,
        To praise thy Name:
  That, if I chance to hold my peace,
  These stones to praise thee may not cease.
O let thy blessed SACRIFICE be mine,
And sanctifie this A L T A R to be thine.

George Herbert

star
star
star
s t a r
star
star
star
star
star
star
star
star
steer

Ian Hamilton Finlay

The Critical Putt

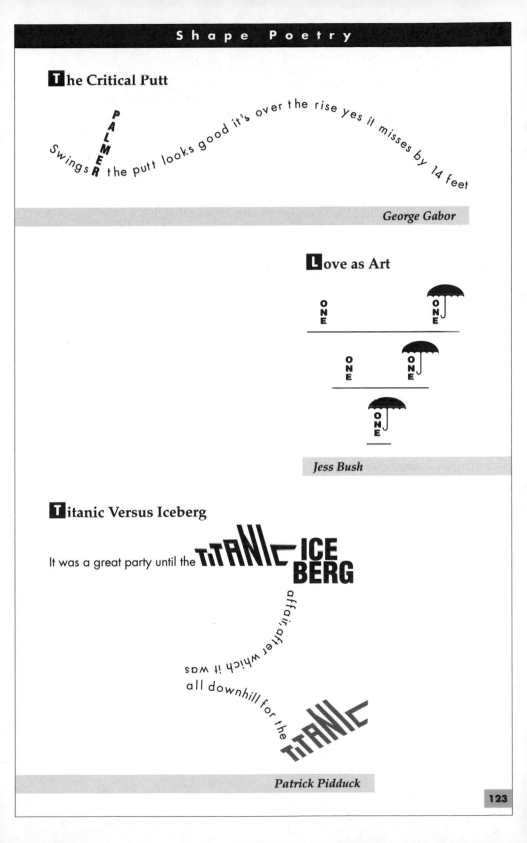

Swings **PALMER** the putt looks good it's over the rise yes it misses by 14 feet

George Gabor

Love as Art

ONE ONE
ONE ONE
ONE

Jess Bush

Titanic Versus Iceberg

It was a great party until the **TITANIC ICE BERG** affair, after which it was all downhill for the **TITANIC**

Patrick Pidduck

Edward Estlin Cummings (1894-1962) created poetry for the eye as well as the ear. Some of his poems, such as "!blac" and "mortals)" are almost kinetic—they appear to move.

Cummings broke from the conventions of proper word order and the correct use of parts of speech, spacing, and upper case and lower case letters.

He used diction, punctuation, form, and spelling in innovative and experimental ways.

In decoding *cummingese* give special attention to spacing and word fragments.

mortals)

climbi
    ng i
    nto eachness begi
    n
dizzily
    swingthings
of speeds of
trapeze gush somersaults
open ing
     hes shes
&meet&
    swoop
       fully is are ex
           quisite theys of re
turn
   a
   n
   d
fall which now drop who all dreamlike

(im

e. e. cummings

cummingese = a new syntax
= "the algebra of the heart"

                         r-p-o-p-h-e-s-s-a-g-r
                    who
          a)s w(e loo)k
          upnowgath
                    PPEGORHRASS
                                   eringint(o-
          aThe):l
                eA
                  !p:
          S   a
                          (r
          rIvInG   .gRrEaPsPhOs)
                                          to
          rea(be)rran(com)gi(e)ngly
          ,grasshopper;

          e. e. cummings

!blac
k
agains
t

(whi)

te sky
?t
rees whic
h fr

om droppe

d

,
le
af

a:;go

e
s wh
IrlI
n

·g

e. e. cummings

maybe god

is a child
's hand)very carefully
bring
-ing
to you and to
me(and quite with
out crushing)the

papery weightless diminutive

world
with a hole in
it out
of which demons with wings would be streaming if
something had(maybe they couldn't
agree)not happened(and floating-
ly int

o

e. e. cummings

Understanding *cummingese*!
• partial translations of the poems on the next page

12

When reading cummings, read what is in the parentheses at the same instant that you read the words outside the parentheses.

(look)
(no more)
once upon
a time two
old men
sit
dream

Why does the poem conclude with the word fragment "am"?

I

Observe in this poem about loneliness how the world walks by in twos.

How many ways does the poet say one?

VIII

At a political meeting…
Read the poem phonetically.

(applause)
"fellow
citizens"
(a pause)

The politician has nothing to say, but with their paws, they clap.

"one" viewed in silhouette

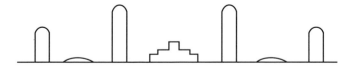

•• 4 poems by e. e. cummings

12

tw

o o
ld
o

nce upo

n
a(
n

o mo

re
)time
me

n

sit(l
oo
k)dre

am

I

l(a

le
af
fa

ll

s)
one
l

iness

VIII

applaws)

"fell

ow
sit
isn'ts"

(a paw s

one
  t
   hi
    s
snowflake
(a
  li
    ght
     in
  g)
is upon a gra
v
es
t
one

- witty, ingenious, eye-pleasing
- has the potential to bridge linguistic barriers
- a return to the poem as picture

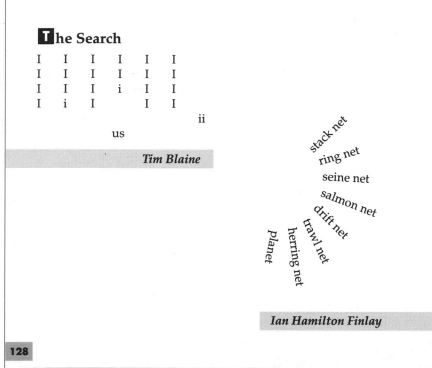

```
elApfelAp     pfelApfelAp
lApfelApfelApfelApfelApfelA
pfelApfelApfelApfelApfelApfel
elApfelApfelApfelApfelApfelApf
ApfelApfelApfelApfelApfelApfel
elApfelApfelApfelApfelApfelAp
pfelApfelApfelApfelApfelApfr
ApfelApfelApfelApfelApfel/
elApfelApfelWurmApfelA
felApfelApfelApfelApf
pfelApfelApfelApfe'
ApfelApfelApfelA
elApfe' ApfelAr
```

Reinhard Döhl

The Search

```
I   I   I   I   I   I
I   I   I   I   I   I
I   I   I   i   I   I
I   i   I       I   I
                        ii
        us
```

Tim Blaine

stack net
ring net
seine net
salmon net
drift net
trawl net
herring net
planet

Ian Hamilton Finlay

128

Wind

```
          w       w
      d       i
    n     n     n
  i     d     i     d
w                   w
```

Eugen Gomringer

Genetics

	B	BA
b	Bb	BAb
by	Bby	BAby

Joe Tripodi

WAN
DO
TREE
FEAR
FIFE
SEEKS
SIPHON
EAT
NEIGHING
DEN
ELEPHAN'
TWIRL

Bob Cobbing

Lunch Counter

```
    un      c       h
```

sHE

ABC
TAXI

E. J. Barry

129

Love is...

laugh laugh
lovers lovers
love is a love is a
love is a bit love is a bit
love is a bitter love is a bitter
love is a bitter mist love is a bitter mist
love is a bitter mystery love is a bitter mystery
love is a bitter mystery love is a bitter mystery
love is a bitter mist love is a bitter mist
love is a bitter love is a bitter
love is a bit love is a bit
love is a love is a
lovers lovers
laugh laugh

Reinhard Döhl

bebe coca cola
babe cola
bebe coca
babe cola caco
caco
cola
cloaca

Decio Pignatari

Pendulum

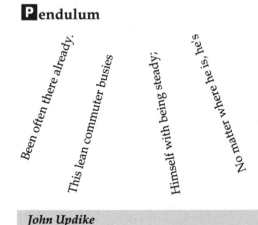

Been often there already.
This lean commuter busies
Himself with being steady;
No matter where he is, he's

John Updike

The Saga of the Auto Industry

```
AMERICA
AMERIC
AMERI
AMER
AME
AM
AN
PAN
APAN
JAPAN
```

Nicholas Harrington

Silencio

```
silencio   silencio   silencio
silencio   silencio   silencio
silencio              silencio
silencio   silencio   silencio
silencio   silencio   silencio
```

Eugen Gomringer

treepoem

how   we   turn   out   to   be   related

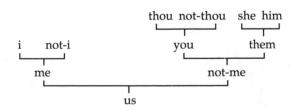

Dom Sylvester Houédard

131

Computer poetry is regular, symmetrical, mathematical. You select a word or phrase and create a readout. The letters are always in the same place on each line.

WATCH YOUR TELEVISION

```
    A                   L
                U
      C
                              I S
    T   H           E
        H           E L
  W                 E
                        E       N
                          V I S I O N
                U
      C
      " H           E L E V I S I O N "
```

Paul O'Neil

MADMEN

```
MA
MAD  E
      ME
      ME
MAD  E
   ADMEN
   ADMEN
MAD  E
MA
   A  MEN !
```

E. J. Barry

LISTENING TO PICTURES

```
    S
   I
 L
      E
        N
                        C
      E
```

Thomas O'Donnell

INDIVIDUALIZATION

```
I                       I
        D U A L
I
```

Greg Dosman

APARTHEID

```
A
  PART
        H -
A     T E.
```

Chris Perry

SMOKING

```
SMOK I N
SMOK I
SMOK
SMO
SM
   " O
    O"
```

E. J. Barry

The Nine Ages of Man

(A poem in one line, to be read aloud.)

Not old enough to know better

```
     "      "     "    "      "
  "    "     "    "     "
       "      "    "    "
  "    "      "
       "      "
  "     "
        "
  "
```

F. Emerson Andrews

SOLITARY CONFINEMENT

```
      I
          A                        M
          A
S O L                       E
```

Paul Flanagan

Several writers work independently to create their own computer poems. Each writer takes the same word or phrase as a starting point.

The editor(s) arrange the different poems into one readout, thus creating a corporate computer poem.

```
T E L E C O N F E R E N C I N G

T E L E      —  R          I N G
                           I
                           C
                              N -

        O
        O N   E

               R          I N G !
               R          I N G !
  "E L    O ?"
          "F          I -
           R E !"

    L    O          N G

               R          I N G
  E   E      E   E
        C O   F          I N
```

Mike Letros   John Marshall
Sean Gamble   Sean Moffitt

```
P O R S C H E   O R   B I C Y C L E

        R                I C -
            H
                O R
  P O            O R

  P   R                I C        E
        S   H E
            H            I
                O R
                                L -
                O

                    B    Y    E
                O R
                    B I

        $        O R            ¢
        $
        $
```

Gino Totera   Anthony Cristillo
Dan Desmarais   Mark McLarney

```
SPLINTERING THE ATOM
                 E   IN-
     S          TE   IN
     SPLI   T              THE   ATOM
                          THE
                                     A
     S
     S                                       !
           N
               E R
                      G
                                         TO
     SPLI   T
                          THE
               E R        T H
                                     A
     SP   I   T
                      I N
                          THE
                      I
                          HE  AT
                  I N
                          THE
     S     T   R      E  AT
         L INT
         I N
                          THE
                                  ATOM
         P   IN        G              !
```

Mark Fisher   Greg James
Mark Fisher   Steve Boyd
Fulvio Ciano   George Longo

```
THE    ALGEBRA  OF   THE  HEART
                          HEAR
                   THE
                O    TH    E  R
 H E
 H E                       HE   R
                           HE   R
 H E              +         HE   R
 H      E       +++   HE         R
 T              O -
         GE           THE        R
```

Jan Krasnodebski   Alan Grozelle

A good poet is someone who manages, in a lifetime of standing out in thunderstorms, to be struck by lightning five or six times; a dozen or two dozen times and he is great.

Robin Skelton

Milton Acorn
Margaret Atwood
Roo Borson
Mary Di Michele
Anne Hébert
D. G. Jones
A. M. Klein
Irving Layton
Dorothy Livesay
Gwendolyn MacEwen
Jay Macpherson
Alden Nowlan
Michael Ondaatje
P. K. Page
Al Pittman
E. J. Pratt
Al Purdy
James Reaney
Miriam Waddington
Tom Wayman
Phyllis Webb
Dale Zieroth

July Creatures

After the dim blue rain
swarms of innocent flying things
(green things, curly-bodied things,
things shaped like an arrowhead)
tiny with outsize wings

go wherever the wind wobbles
among pinwheeling swallows
and meet uncomprehended harm
in blond thickets on my forearm.

Milton Acorn

The Miner's Wife

The pit's above and down below the town,
And every day the man I love goes down.
It's not the pleasantest place to spend the day
But he must go down to earn his pay.

The pit's as black as night…as black as death.
It keeps on breathing out its coaley breath.
Tho I eternally wash it's always there
Until I'd give my soul for good clean air.

But half my Johnny's life's down in that dirt,
Where every step you go some man's been hurt.
It's sure I am he'll be carried out some day,
But he must go down to earn his pay.

The coal's been there a hundred million years,
Like sunshine hidden in a sepulchre.
It's strange my Johnny works to bring it up
Then comes out blacker than the devil's pup.

The man I love is sunshine all himself;
He makes this land but doesn't own its wealth.
He's a working man…and what's there more to say?
So he must go down to earn his pay.

Milton Acorn

Dream 2: Brian the Still-Hunter

The man I saw in the forest
used to come to our house
every morning, never said anything;
I learned from the neighbours later
he once tried to cut his throat.

I found him at the end of the path
sitting on a fallen tree
cleaning his gun.

There was no wind;
around us the leaves rustled.   10

He said to me:
I kill because I have to

but every time I aim, I feel
my skin grow fur
my head heavy with antlers
and during the stretched instant
the bullet glides on its thread of speed
my soul runs innocent as hooves.

Is God just to his creatures?

I die more often than many.   20

He looked up and I saw
the white scar made by the hunting knife
around his neck.

When I woke
I remembered: he has been gone
twenty years and not heard from.

Margaret Atwood

It Is Dangerous to Read Newspapers

While I was building neat
castles in the sandbox,
the hasty pits were
filling with bulldozed corpses

and as I walked to the school
washed and combed, my feet
stepping on the cracks in the cement
detonated red bombs.

Now I am grownup
and literate, and I sit in my chair   10
as quietly as a fuse

and the jungles are flaming, the under-
brush is charged with soldiers,
the names on the difficult
maps go up in smoke.

I am the cause, I am a stockpile of chemical
toys, my body
is a deadly gadget,
I reach out in love, my hands are guns,
my good intentions are completely lethal.   20

Even my
passive eyes transmute
everything I look at to the pocked
black and white of a war photo,
how
can I stop myself

It is dangerous to read newspapers.

Each time I hit a key
on my electric typewriter,
speaking of peaceful trees   30

another village explodes.

Margaret Atwood

Grey Glove

Among branches
a bird lands fluttering,
a soft grey glove
with a heart.

The land at twilight.
Swamp of black mist.
A first planet. A swordtip.
The bird chanting
in a jail of darkness.

This is the last unclassified bird,
the one one never sees,
but hears when alone, walking.

You can see how far I've gone
not to speak of you.
Birds have made a simple bargain
with the land.

The only song I know
is the one I see with my eyes,
the one I'd give up my eyes
in order for you to hear.

Roo Borson

The Wind, Growing Up

The wind. It comes at night,
trying to claw the house apart.
It goes at all the windows.
The windows shudder in their frames.
The wind wants you to come out and be blown
forever through a world moving too fast
for you to see it. The way the wind sees it.
So what if you lie under the covers and shiver?
The same wind goes through your lungs, through and through...
through and through.

Roo Borson

As in the Beginning

A man has two hands and when one
gets caught on the belt and his fingers
are amputated and then patched
he cannot work. His hands are insured
however so he gets some money
for the work his hands have done before.
If he loses a finger he gets a flat sum
of $250 for each digit &/or $100 for a joint
missing for the rest of his stay on earth,
like an empty stool at a beggar's banquet.   10
When the hands are my father's hands
it makes me cry although my pen must keep scratching
its head across the page of another night.
To you my father is a stranger
and perhaps you think the insurance paid is enough.

Give me my father's hands when they are not broken
and swollen,
give me my father's hands, young again,
and holding the hands of my mother,
give me my father's hands still brown and uncallused,   20
beautiful hands that broke bread for us at table,
hands as smooth as marble and naked as the morning,
give me hands without a number tattooed at the wrist,
without the copper sweat of clinging change,
give my father's hands as they were in the beginning,
whole,
open,
warm
and without fear.

Mary Di Michele

Les Petites Villes

Je te donnerai de petites villes
De toutes petites villes tristes.

Les petites villes dans nos mains
Sont plus austères que des jouets
Mais aussi faciles à manier.

Je joue avec les petites villes.
Je les renverse.
Pas un homme ne s'en échappe
Ni une fleur ni un enfant.

Les petites villes sont désertes   10
Et livrées dans nos mains.

J'écoute, l'oreille contre les portes
J'approche une à une toutes les portes,
De mon oreille.

Les maisons ressemblent à des coquillages muets
Qui ne gardent dans leurs spirales glacées
Aucune rumeur de vent
Aucune rumeur d'eau.

Les parcs et les jardins sont morts
Les jeux alignés   20
Ainsi que dans un musée.

Je ne sais pas où l'on a mis
Les corps figés des oiseaux.

Les rues sont sonores de silence.
L'écho du silence est lourd
Plus lourd
Qu'aucune parole de menace ou d'amour

Mais voici qu'à mon tour
J'abandonne les petites villes de mon enfance.
Je te les offre   30
Dans la plénitude
De leur solitude.

Comprends-tu bien le présent redoutable?
Je te donne d'étranges petites villes tristes,
Pour le songe.

Anne Hébert

The Little Towns

I shall give you the little towns
The poor sad little towns,

The little towns cupped in our palms
More exigent than toys
As easy to the hand.

I play with the little towns,
I turn them over
Never a man escapes them
No flower, no child.

The little towns are empty—   10
Given into our hands.

I listen, my ear to the doors
I lean to the doors, one by one,
With my ear...

O the houses are dumb sea-shells—
No longer in the frozen spiral
Any sound of the wind
Any sound of water.

Dead, the parks and the gardens
The games are all put to sleep   20
In a dead museum.

I cannot tell where they have put
The deathstill bodies of the birds.

The streets resound with silence
The echo of their silence is a weight of lead
More leaden
Than any words of menace or of love.

And here am I too, in my turn
Forsaking the little towns of my childhood...
I offer them to you   30
In all the infinite depth
Of their loneliness.

Now do you grasp the dangerous gift?
I have given you the strange sad little towns
For your own imagining.

Translated from the French by John Glassco

Anne Hébert

On the 24th of May

Six cows
lie
or kneel
in the green grass
like badly built tents
they flap
an ear
or tail
to keep off the flies
they look out
from unnecessarily
large eyes
at the bright
automobiles
driving northward
and are profoundly
unmoved

D. G. Jones

Forget-me-nots

riot like water down
the bank these hot days
when nothing happens
white lace blue lace
of silent waterfalls
forget-me-nots forget-
me-nots what was there
to remember or forget

D. G. Jones

A Portrait of Anne Hébert

The sunlight, here and there
touches a table

and a draught at the window
announces your presence

You take your place in the room
without fuss

your delicate bones
your frock
have the grace of disinterested passion

Words are arrayed   10
like surgical instruments
neatly in trays

deftly, you make an incision
probing
the obscure disease

your sensibility
has the sure fingers of the blind

each decision
cuts like a scalpel
through tangled emotion   20

you define
the morbid tissue, laying it bare

like a tatter of lace
dark
on the paper

D. G. Jones

Heirloom

My father bequeathed me no wide estates;
No keys and ledgers were my heritage;
Only some holy books with *yahrzeit* dates
Writ mournfully upon a blank front page—

Books of the Baal Shem Tov, and of his wonders;
Pamphlets upon the devil and his crew;
Prayers against road demons, witches, thunders;
And sundry other tomes for a good Jew.

Beautiful: though no pictures on them, save
The scorpion crawling on a printed track;
The Virgin floating on a scriptural wave,
Square letters twinkling in the Zodiac.

The snuff left on this page, now brown and old,
The tallow stains of midnight liturgy—
These are my coat of arms, and these unfold
My noble lineage, my proud ancestry!

And my tears, too, have stained this heirloomed ground,
When reading in these treatises some weird
Miracle, I turned a leaf and found
A white hair fallen from my father's beard.

A. M. Klein

Of Nothing at All:
Orders

Muffle the wind;
Silence the clock;
Muzzle the mice;
Curb the small talk;
Cure the hinge-squeak;
Banish the thunder.
Let me sit silent,
Let me wonder.

A. M. Klein

A poem is not a destination, it is a point of departure. The destination is determined by the reader. The poet's function is but to point direction. A poem is not the conflagration complete, it is the first kindling.

A. M. Klein

The Well-Wrought Urn

"What would you do
if I suddenly died?"

"Write a poem to you."

"Would you mourn for me?"

"Certainly," I sighed.

"For a long time?"

"That depends."

"On what?"

"The poem's excellence," I replied.

Irving Layton

A Spider Danced a Cosy Jig

A spider danced a cosy jig
Upon a frail trapeze;
And from a far-off clover field
An ant was heard to sneeze.

And kings that day were wise and just,
And stones began to bleed;
A dead man rose to tell a tale,
A bigot changed his creed.

The stableboy forgot his pride,
The queen confessed an itch;
And lo! more wonderful than all,
The poor man blessed the rich.

Irving Layton

Success

I've always wanted
to write
a poem
with the word
'zeugma'
in it.

Now I've done it!

Irving Layton

Fire and Reason

I cannot shut out the night—
Nor its sharp clarity.

The many blinds we draw,
You and I,
The many fires we light
Can never quite obliterate
The irony of stars,
The deliberate moon,
The last, unsolved finality of night.

Dorothy Livesay

Green Rain

I remember long veils of green rain
Feathered like the shawl of my grandmother—
Green from the half-green of the spring trees
Waving in the valley.

I remember the road
Like the one which leads to my grandmother's house,
A warm house, with green carpets,
Geraniums, a trilling canary
And shining horse-hair chairs;
And the silence, full of the rain's falling
Was like my grandmother's parlour
Alive with herself and her voice, rising and falling—
Rain and wind intermingled.

I remember on that day
I was thinking only of my love
And of my love's house.
But now I remember the day
As I remember my grandmother.
I remember the rain as the feathery fringe of her shawl.

Dorothy Livesay

147

Inside the Great Pyramid

all day the narrow shaft
received us; everyone
came out sweating and
gasping for air, and one
old man collapsed
upon a stair;
        I thought:
the fact that it has stood
so long
is no guarantee   10
it will stand today,
but went in anyway
and heard when I was
halfway up a long
low rumbling like
the echo of ancient stones
first straining to their place;
        I thought:
we have made this, we
have made *this*.   20
I scrambled out into
the scandalous sun and saw
the desert was an hourglass
we had forgotten to invert,
a tasselled camel falling
to his knees, the River
filling the great waterclock
of earth.

Gwendolyn MacEwen

The Children Are Laughing

It is monday and the children are laughing
The children are laughing; they believe they are princes
They wear no shoes; they believe they are princes
And their filthy kingdom heaves up behind them

The filthy city heaves up behind them
They are older than I am, their feet are shoeless
They have lived a thousand years; the children are laughing
The children are laughing and their death is upon them

I have cried in the city (the children are laughing)
I have worn many colours (the children are laughing)
They are older than I am, their death is upon them
I will wear no shoes when the princes are dying

Gwendolyn MacEwen

The Fisherman

The world was first a private park
Until the angel, after dark,
Scattered afar to wests and easts
The lovers and the friendly beasts.

And later still a home-made boat
Contained Creation set afloat,
No rift nor leak that might betray
The creatures to a hostile day.

But now beside the midnight lake
One single fisher sits awake
And casts and fights and hauls to land
A myriad forms upon the sand.

Old Adam on the naming-day
Blessed each and let it slip away:
The fisher of the fallen mind
Sees no occasion to be kind,

But on his catch proceeds to sup;
Then bends, and at one slurp sucks up
The lake and all that therein is
To slake that hungry gut of his,

Then whistling makes for home and bed
As the last morning breaks in red;
But God the Lord with patient grin
Lets down his hook and hoicks him in.

Jay Macpherson

The Third Eye

Of three eyes I would still give two for one.
The third eye clouds: its light is nearly gone.
The two saw green, saw sky, saw people pass:
The third eye saw through order like a glass
To concentrate, refine and rarify
And make a Cosmos of miscellany.
Sight, world and all to save alive that one
Fading so fast! Ah love, its light is done.

Jay Macpherson

Two Strangers

Two strangers, one of whom was I,
shook with a rabbit's queasy cry
suppressed by the quick hangman's hood
in the forest of gallows wood.

For one the child-like scream of death
resounded in his tightened breath,
he knew only the air had cried,
the voice itself had died, had died.

For one the ghostly cry brought back
the exultation of the track.
He tasted in his rearing will
the salt of the climactic kill.

For that breath's space there in the trees
they burned with their identities.
Then finding every echo gone,
still saying nothing, they walked on.

Alden Nowlan

The Execution

On the night of the execution
a man at the door
mistook me for the coroner.
"Press," I said.

But he didn't understand. He led me
into the wrong room
where the sheriff greeted me:
"You're late, Padre."

"You're wrong," I told him. "I'm Press."
"Yes, of course, Reverend Press."   10
We went down a stairway.

"Ah, Mr. Ellis," said the Deputy.
"Press!" I shouted. But he shoved me
through a black curtain.
The lights were so bright
I couldn't see the faces
of the men sitting
opposite. But, thank God, I thought
they can see me!

"Look!" I cried. "Look at my face!   20
Doesn't anybody know me?"

Then a hood covered my head.
"Don't make it harder for us," the hangman whispered.

The Bull Moose

Down from the purple mist of trees on the mountain,
lurching through forests of white spruce and cedar,
stumbling through tamarack swamps,
came the bull moose
to be stopped at last by a pole-fenced pasture.

Too tired to turn or, perhaps, aware
there was no place left to go, he stood with the cattle.
They, scenting the musk of death, seeing his great head
like the ritual mask of a blood god, moved to the other end
of the field, and waited.   10

The neighbours heard of it, and by afternoon
cars lined the road. The children teased him
with alder switches and he gazed at them
like an old, tolerant collie. The women asked
if he could have escaped from a Fair.

The oldest man in the parish remembered seeing
a gelded moose yoked with an ox for plowing.
The young men snickered and tried to pour beer
down his throat, while their girl friends took their pictures.

And the bull moose let them stroke his tick-ravaged flanks,   20
let them pry open his jaws with bottles, let a giggling girl
plant a little purple cap
of thistles on his head.

When the wardens came, everyone agreed it was a shame
to shoot anything so shaggy and cuddlesome.
He looked liked the kind of pet
women put to bed with their sons.

So they held their fire. But just as the sun dropped in the river
the bull moose gathered his strength
like a scaffolded king, straightened and lifted his horns   30
so that even the wardens backed away as they raised their rifles.
When he roared, people ran to their cars. All the young men
leaned on their automobile horns as he toppled.

Alden Nowlan

Signature

The car carried him
racing the obvious moon
beating in the trees like a white bird.

Difficult to make words sing
around your appendix.
The obvious upsets me,
everyone has scars which crawl
into the mystery of swimming trunks.

I was the first appendix in my family;
my brother who was given the stigma   10
of a rare blood type,
proved to have ulcers instead.

The rain fell like applause as I approached the hospital.

It takes seven seconds she said,
strapped my feet,
entered my arm.
I stretched all senses
on FIVE
the room closed on me like an eyelid.

At night the harmonica plays,   20
a whistler joins in respect.
I am a sweating marble saint
full of demerol and sleeping pills.
A man in the armour of shining plaster
walks to my door, then past.
Imagine the rain
falling like white bees on the sidewalk
imagine Snyder
high on poetry and mountains

Three floors down   30
my appendix
swims in a jar

O world, I shall be buried all over Ontario

Michael Ondaatje

A House Divided

This midnight breathing
heaves with no sensible rhythm,
is fashioned by no metronome.
Your body, eager
for the extra yard of bed,
reconnoitres and outflanks;
I bend in peculiar angles.

This nightly battle is fought with subtleties:
you get pregnant, I'm sure,
just for extra ground
—immune from kicks now.

Inside you now's another,
thrashing like a fish,
swinging, fighting
for its inch already.

Michael Ondaatje

Fabulous Shadow

They fished me from this Quebec river
the face blurred glass, bones of wing
draping my body like nets
in a patterned butterfly

and peeled green weed from scorched shoulders
and the dried wax from my thighs

Michael Ondaatje

T-Bar

Relentless, black on white, the cable runs
through metal arches up the mountain side.
At intervals giant pickaxes are hung
on long hydraulic springs. The skiers ride
propped by the axehead, twin automatons
supported by its handle, one each side.

In twos they move slow motion up the steep
incision in the mountain. Climb. Climb.
Somnambulists, bolt upright in their sleep
their phantom poles swung lazily behind,
while to the right, the empty T-bars keep
in mute descent, slow monstrous jigging time.

Captive the skiers now and innocent,
wards of eternity, each pair alone.
They mount the easy vertical ascent,
pass through successive arches, bride and groom,
as through successive naves, are newly wed
participants in some recurring dream.

So do they move forever. Clocks are broken.
In zones of silence they grow tall and slow,
inanimate dreamers, mild and gentle-spoken
blood-brothers of the haemophilic snow
until the summit breaks and they awaken
imagos from the stricture of the tow.

Jerked from her chrysalis the sleeping bride
suffers too sudden freedom like a pain.
The dreaming bridegroom severed from her side
singles her out, the old wound aches again.
Uncertain, lost, upon a wintry height
these two, not separate, but no longer one.

Now clocks begin to peck and sing. The slow
extended minute like a rubber band
contracts to catapult them through the snow
in tandem trajectory while behind
etching the sky-line, obdurate and slow
the spastic T-bars pivot and descend.

P. K. Page

Faith Healer

They come from as far away
as Stephenville Crossing
to this tent
this temple
hobbling
bent
broken
pock marked
the whole ignoble mess
of west shore humanity   10
crammed into canvas
waiting
hoping
praying
that this time perhaps
God willing
their turn will come
and why not
haven't they seen miracles before

wasn't it this same man   20
this saint
who last year
laid hands upon a cripple
and God Almighty just like that
weren't the crutches thrown off
and didn't the fellow begin to dance
praising God all up and down the aisles

and hadn't they heard about the cures
last week at North Sydney too
hadn't the posters proclaimed it all   30
and wasn't this the self same man
and wasn't it only right
that perhaps tonight God willing
they'd leave their own
crutches and wheelchairs
pain and twist behind them
and if they weren't chosen
for miracles tonight
then wouldn't there always be next year
to look forward to   40
and perhaps then God willing…

Al Pittman

To a Retarded Child Dancing All Alone in an Asphalt School Yard

Your dizzy dance
young fellow
invites me
like a whirlpool
but when I try
to step
I am suddenly reminded
of my normality
and my feet
become all thumbs

Al Pittman

The Dying Eagle

A light had gone out from his vanquished eyes;
His head was cupped within the hunch of his shoulders;
His feathers were dull and bedraggled; the tips
Of his wings sprawled down to the edge of his tail.
He was old, yet it was not his age
Which made him roost on the crags
Like a rain-drenched raven
On the branch of an oak in November.
Nor was it the night, for there was an hour
To go before sunset. An iron had entered   10
His soul which bereft him of pride and of realm,
Had struck him today; for up to noon
That crag had been his throne.
Space was his empire, bounded only
By forest and sky and the flowing horizons.
He had outfought, outlived all his rivals,
And the eagles that now were poised over glaciers
Or charting the coastal outlines of clouds
Were his by descent: they had been tumbled
Out of their rocky nests by his mate,   20
In the first trial of their fledgeling spins.

Only this morning the eyes of the monarch
Were held in arrest by a silver flash
Shining between two peaks of the ranges—
A sight which galvanized his back,
Bristled the feathers on his neck,
And shot little runnels of dust where his talons
Dug recesses in the granite.
Partridge? Heron? Falcon? Eagle?
Game or foe? He would reconnoitre.   30

Catapulting from the ledge,
He flew at first with rapid beat,
Level, direct; then with his grasp
Of spiral strategy in fight,
He climbed the orbit
With swift and easy undulations,
And reached position where he might
Survey the bird—for bird it was;
But such a bird as never flew
Between the heavens and the earth   40

Since pterodactyls, long before
The birth of condors, learned to kill
And drag their carrion up the Andes.

The eagle stared at the invader,
Marked the strange bat-like shadow moving
In leagues over the roofs of the world,
Across the passes and moraines,
Darkening the vitriol blue of the mountain lakes.
Was it a flying dragon? Head,
Body and wings, a tail fan-spread   50
And taut like his own before the strike;
And there in front two whirling eyes
That took unshuttered
The full blaze of the meridian.
The eagle never yet had known
A rival that he would not grapple,
But something in this fellow's length
Of back, his plated glistening shoulders,
Had given him pause. And did that thunder
Somewhere in his throat not argue   60
Lightning in his claws? And then
The speed—was it not double his own?
But what disturbed him most, angered
And disgraced him was the unconcern
With which this supercilious bird
Cut through the aquiline dominion,
Snubbing the ancient suzerain
With extra-territorial insolence,
And disappeared.

So evening found him on the crags again,   70
This time with sloven shoulders
And nerveless claws.
Dusk had outridden the sunset by an hour
To haunt his unhorizoned eyes.
And soon his flock flushed with the chase
Would be returning, threading their glorious curves
Up through the crimson archipelagoes
Only to find him there—
Deaf to the mighty symphony of wings,
And brooding   80
Over the lost empire of the peaks.

E. J. Pratt

Joe Barr

In a grey town of seven-week days
during an eternal childhood
where I was so miserable sometimes
at being me that I roamed lonely
over the reeking town garbage dump
unable to talk to anyone
locked in my own body
captive of the motionless sun
in an eternal childhood

Old Joe went there too   10
happy as a young dog
pushing the garbage with his stick
grinning like a split orange
telling himself stories all day
the doors of his prison opening
into rooms he couldn't remember
places he couldn't stay
the river providing a green sidewalk
that bore his mind's feet lightly
his days like scraps of colour   20
and the night birds always teaching
him songs that because of his stutter
he never learned to sing

I could have learned from Joe myself
but I never did
not even when gangs of children
followed him down the street
chanting "aw-aw-aw" in mockery
children have for idiots
In a town that looked like a hole   30
torn in blue clouds
where I made-believe myself
into a moonlit grasshopper
and leaped the shadowed boundaries

that bore my mind's feet lightly
forty years ago
In the grey town of memory
the garbage dump is a prison
where people stand like stones
the birds are stuffed and mounted   40
a motionless sun still hangs there
where Joe is a scrap of crimson
when the sun at last goes down

Al Purdy

Winnipeg Seen as a Body of Time and Space

Winnipeg, what once were you. You were,
Your hair was grass by the river ten feet tall,
Your arms were burr oaks and ash leaf maples,
Your backbone was a crooked silver muddy river,
Your thoughts were ravens in flocks, your bones were snow,
Your legs were trails and your blood was a people
    Who did what the stars did and the sun.

Then what were you? You were cracked enamel like
Into parishes and strips that come down to the river.
Convents were built, the river lined with nuns   10
Praying and windmills turning and your people
Had a blood that did what a star did and a Son.

Then on top of you fell
A Boneyard wrecked auto gent, his hair
Made of rusted car door handles, his fingernails
Of red Snowflake Pastry signs, his belly
Of buildings downtown; his arms of sewers,
His nerves electric wires, his mouth a telephone,
His backbone—a cracked cement street. His heart
An orange pendulum bus crawling with the human fleas   20
Of a so-so civilization—half gadget, half flesh—
    I don't know what I would have instead—
    And they did what they did more or less.

James Reaney

Advice to the Young

1

keep bees and
grow asparagus,
watch the tides
and listen to the
wind instead of
the politicians
make up your own
stories and believe
them if you want to
live the good life.   10

2

All rituals
are instincts
never fully
trust them
study to im-
prove biology
with reason.

3

Digging trenches
for asparagus
is good for the   20
muscles and
waiting for the
plants to settle
teaches patience
to those who are
usually in too
much of a hurry.

4

There is morality
in bee-keeping
it teaches how   30
not to be afraid
of the bee swarm
it teaches how
not to be afraid of
finding new places
and building them
all over again.

Miriam Waddington

Picketing Supermarkets

Because all this food is grown in the store
do not take the leaflet.
Cabbages, broccoli and tomatoes
are raised at night in the aisles.
Milk is brewed in the rear storage areas.
Beef produced in vats in the basement.
Do not take the leaflet.
Peanut butter and soft drinks
are made fresh each morning by store employees.
Our oranges and grapes   10
are so fine and round
that when held up to the lights they cast no shadow.
Do not take the leaflet.

And should you take one
do not believe it.
This chain of stores has no connection
with anyone growing food someplace else.
How could we have an effect on local farmers?
Do not believe it.

The sound here is Muzak, for your enjoyment.   20
It is not the sound of children crying.
There *is* a lady offering samples
to mark Canada Cheese Month.
There is no dark-skinned man with black hair beside her
wanting to show you the inside of a coffin.
You would not have to look if there was.
And there are no Nicaraguan heroes
in any way connected with the bananas.
Pay no attention to these people.
The manager is a citizen.   30
All this food is grown in the store.

Tom Wayman

Poets are the unacknowledged legislators of the world.

Percy Bysshe Shelley

And in Our Time

A world flew in my mouth with our first kiss
and its wings were dipped in all the flavours of grief.
Oh my darling, tell me, what can love mean in such a world,
and what can we or any lovers hold in this immensity
of hate and broken things?
Now it is down, down, that's where your kiss travels me,
and, as a world tumbling shocks the theories of spheres,
so this love is like falling glass shaking with stars
the air which tomorrow, or even today, will be
a slow, terrible movement of scars.

Phyllis Webb

Sitting

The degree of nothingness
is important:
to sit emptily
in the sun
receiving fire
that is the way
to mend
an extraordinary world,
sitting perfectly
still
and only
remotely human.

Phyllis Webb

from Non Linear

An instant of white roses.
        Inbreathing.
A black butterfly's
        twitch and determined
collapse on a yellow round.

Phyllis Webb

The Hunters of the Deer

The ten men will dress in white
to match the snow and leave the last
farmhouse and the last woman, going
north into the country of the deer. It
is from there, and from past there, that
the wind begins that can shake
every window in the house and leaves
the woman wishing she had moved away
five years and five children ago.

During the day the father of her children   10
will kill from a distance. With the others
he will track and drive each bush
and at least once he will kill before
they stop and come together for
coffee in scratched quart jars. And
sometimes the November sun will glint
on the rifles propped together in the snow.

In the evening, as they skin and gut,
they talk about the one that ran three
miles on a broken leg and the bitch wolf   20
they should have shot and how John
the bachelor likes eating more than
hunting and they pass the whiskey
around to keep warm. In the house
the woman makes a meal from pork.

These men are hunters and later,
standing in bright electrically lighted
rooms they are embarrassed with the
blood on their clothes and although the
woman nods and seems to understand,   30
she grows restless with their talk.
She has not heard another woman in fourteen days.

And when they leave, the man sleeps
and his children sleep while the woman
waits and listens for the howling of
wolves. To the north, the grey
she-wolf smells the red snow and howls.
She also is a hunter of the deer.
Tonight, while other hunters sleep, she
drinks at the throat.

Dale Zieroth

William Blake
Robert Burns
Emily Dickinson
T. S. Eliot
Gerard Manley Hopkins
A. E. Housman
John Keats
Amy Lowell
William Shakespeare
Walt Whitman
William Wordsworth
William Butler Yeats

> *A great poem is for ages and ages in common and for all degrees and complexions and all departments and sects and for a woman as much as a man and a man as much as a woman. A great poem is no finish to a man or woman but rather a beginning.*
> **Walt Whitman**

> *Literature is news that STAYS news.*
> **Ezra Pound**

> *All poetry is experimental poetry.*
> **Wallace Stevens**

The Shepherd

How sweet is the Shepherd's sweet lot!
From the morn to the evening he strays;
He shall follow his sheep all the day,
And his tongue shall be fillèd with praise.

For he hears the lamb's innocent call,
And he hears the ewe's tender reply;
He is watchful while they are in peace,
For they know when their Shepherd is nigh.

William Blake

The Chimney Sweeper

When my mother died I was very young,
And my father sold me while yet my tongue
Could scarcely cry "'weep! 'weep! 'weep! 'weep!"
So your chimneys I sweep, & in soot I sleep.

There's little Tom Dacre, who cried when his head,
That curl'd like a lamb's back, was shav'd: so I said
"Hush, Tom! never mind it, for when your head's bare
You know that the soot cannot spoil your white hair."

And so he was quiet, & that very night,
As Tom was a-sleeping, he had such a sight!—
That thousands of sweepers, Dick, Joe, Ned, & Jack,
Were all of them lock'd up in coffins of black.

And by came an Angel who had a bright key,
And he open'd the coffins & set them all free;
Then down a green plain leaping, laughing, they run,
And wash in a river, and shine in the Sun.

Then naked & white, all their bags left behind,
They rise upon clouds and sport in the wind;
And the Angel told Tom, if he'd be a good boy,
He'd have God for his father, & never want joy.

And so Tom awoke; and we rose in the dark,
And got with our bags & our brushes to work.
Tho' the morning was cold, Tom was happy & warm;
So if all do their duty they need not fear harm.

William Blake

- The manuscript of "The Tyger" shows the significant changes Blake made as he composed this famous poem.

- Words in italics represent words that were crossed out on the manuscript.

The Tyger

1. Tyger Tyger burning bright
   In the forests of the night
   What immortal hand & eye
              or
   Could frame thy fearful symmetry
   Dare

2. *In what* distant deeps or skies
   Burnt in
   Burnt the fire of thine eyes
   The cruel
   On what wings dare he aspire
   What the hand dare sieze the fire

3. And what shoulder & what art
   Could twist the sinews of thy heart
   And when thy heart began to beat
   What dread hand & what dread feet

   Could fetch it from the furnace deep
   And in thy horrid ribs dare steep
   In the well of sanguine woe
   In what clay & in what mould
   Were thy eyes of fury rolld

4. *What* the hammer *what* the chain
   Where   *where*
   In what furnace was thy brain
   What the anvil What *the* *arm*
                       arm
                       grasp
                       clasp
                  dread grasp
   Could its deadly terrors *clasp*
   Dare   *grasp*
                   clasp

   Burnt in distant deeps or skies
   The cruel fire of thine eyes
   Could heart descend or wings aspire
   What the hand dare sieze the fire

5. And *did he laugh* his work to see
           dare he *smile*
                laugh
   What the shoulder what the knee
              ankle
   Did he who made the lamb make thee
   Dare
   When the stars threw down their spears
   And waterd heaven with their tears

6. Tyger Tyger burning bright
   In the forests of the night
   What immortal hand & eye
   Dare *form* thy fearful symmetry
         frame

William Blake

The Tyger

Tyger! Tyger! burning bright
In the forests of the night,
What immortal hand or eye
Could frame thy fearful symmetry?

In what distant deeps or skies
Burnt the fire of thine eyes?
On what wings dare he aspire?
What the hand dare sieze the fire?

And what shoulder, & what art,
Could twist the sinews of thy heart?
And when thy heart began to beat,
What dread hand? & what dread feet?

What the hammer? what the chain?
In what furnace was thy brain?
What the anvil? what dread grasp
Dare its deadly terrors clasp?

When the stars threw down their spears,
And water'd heaven with their tears,
Did he smile his work to see?
Did he who made the Lamb make thee?

Tyger! Tyger! burning bright
In the forests of the night,
What immortal hand or eye,
Dare frame thy fearful symmetry?

William Blake

Ah! Sun-Flower

Ah, Sun-flower! weary of time,
Who countest the steps of the sun;
Seeking after that sweet golden clime,
Where the traveller's journey is done;

Where the Youth pined away with desire,
And the pale Virgin shrouded in snow,
Arise from their graves, and aspire
Where my Sun-flower wishes to go.

William Blake

To a Mouse

Wee, sleekit, cowrin', tim'rous beastie,
O, what a panic's in thy breastie!
Thou need na start awa sae hasty
    Wi' bickering brattle!
I wad be laith to rin an' chase thee
    Wi' murd'rin' pattle!   6

I'm truly sorry man's dominion
Has broken nature's social union,
An' justifies that ill opinion
    Which makes thee startle
At me, thy poor, earthborn companion,
    An' fellow mortal!   12

I doubt na, whyles, but thou may thieve;
What then? poor beastie, thou maun live!
A daimen icker in a thrave
    'S a sma' request;
I'll get a blessin' wi' the lave,
    An' never miss 't!   18

Thy wee bit housie, too, in ruin!
It's silly wa's the win's are strewin'!
An' naething, now, to big a new ane,
    O' foggage green!
An' bleak December's winds ensuin',
    Baith snell an' keen!   24

Thou saw the fields laid bare and waste,
An' weary winter comin' fast,
An' cozie here, beneath the blast,
    Thou thought to dwell,
Till crash! the cruel coulter passed
    Out through thy cell.   30

That wee bit heap o' leaves an' stibble
Has cost thee mony a weary nibble!
Now thou's turn'd out, for a' thy trouble,
    But house or hald,
To thole the winter's sleety dribble
    An' cranreuch cauld!   36

But, Mousie, thou art no thy lane
In proving foresight may be vain;
The best laid schemes o' mice an' men
    Gang aft agley,
An' lea'e us nought but grief an' pain,
    For promis'd joy.   42

Still thou art blest, compared wi' me,
The present only toucheth thee;
But och! I backward cast my e'e
    On prospects drear!
An' forward, though I canna see,
    I guess an' fear!   48

Robert Burns

Mary Morison

O Mary, at thy window be,
   It is the wish'd, the trysted hour!
Those smiles and glances let me see
   That make the miser's treasure poor:
   How blythely wad I bide the stoure,
A weary slave frae sun to sun,
   Could I the rich reward secure,
The lovely Mary Morison.

Yestreen when to the trembling string
   The dance gaed thro' the lighted ha',
To thee my fancy took its wing,—
   I sat, but neither heard nor saw:
   Tho' this was fair, and that was braw,
And yon the toast of a' the town,
   I sigh'd, and said amang them a',
"Ye are na Mary Morison."

O Mary, canst thou wreck his peace
   Wha for thy sake wad gladly dee?
Or canst thou break that heart of his,
   Whase only faut is loving thee?
   If love for love thou wiltna gie,
At least be pity to me shown;
   A thought ungentle canna be
The thought o' Mary Morison.

Robert Burns

Hope is a subtle glutton;
    He feeds upon the fair;
And yet, inspected closely,
    What abstinence is there!

His is the halcyon table
    That never seats but one,
And whatsoever is consumed
    The same amounts remain.

Emily Dickinson

Because I could not stop for Death—
He kindly stopped for me—
The Carriage held but just ourselves—
And Immortality.

We slowly drove—He knew no haste,
And I had put away
My labour and my leisure too,
For His Civility—

We passed the School, where Children strove
At Recess—in the Ring—
We passed the Fields of Gazing Grain—
We passed the Setting Sun—

Or rather—He passed Us—
The Dews grew quivering and chill—
For only Gossamer, my Gown—
My Tippet—only Tulle—

We paused before a House that seemed
A Swelling of the Ground—
The Roof was scarcely visible—
The Cornice—in the Ground.

Since then—'tis Centuries—and yet
Feels shorter than the Day
I first surmised the Horses' Heads
Were toward Eternity—

Emily Dickinson

This is my letter to the world,
    That never wrote to me,—
The simple news that Nature told,
    With tender majesty.

Her message is committed
    To hands I cannot see;
For love of her, sweet countrymen,
    Judge tenderly of me!

Emily Dickinson

The Hollow Men

Mistah Kurtz—he dead.

A penny for the Old Guy

I

We are the hollow men
We are the stuffed men
Leaning together
Headpiece filled with straw. Alas!
Our dried voices, when
We whisper together
Are quiet and meaningless
As wind in dry grass
Or rats' feet over broken glass
In our dry cellar   10

Shape without form, shade without colour,
Paralysed force, gesture without motion;

Those who have crossed
With direct eyes, to death's other Kingdom
Remember us—if at all—not as lost
Violent souls, but only
As the hollow men
The stuffed men.

II

Eyes I dare not meet in dreams
In death's dream kingdom   20
These do not appear:

There, the eyes are
Sunlight on a broken column
There, is a tree swinging
And voices are
In the wind's singing
More distant and more solemn
Than a fading star.

Let me be no nearer
In death's dream kingdom   30
Let me also wear
Such deliberate disguises
Rat's coat, crowskin, crossed staves

In a field
Behaving as the wind behaves
No nearer—

Not that final meeting
In the twilight kingdom.

III

This is the dead land
This is cactus land   40
Here the stone images
Are raised, here they receive
The supplication of a dead man's hand
Under the twinkle of a fading star.

Is it like this
In death's other kingdom
Waking alone
At the hour when we are
Trembling with tenderness
Lips that would kiss   50
Form prayers to broken stone.

IV

The eyes are not here
There are no eyes here
In this valley of dying stars
In this hollow valley
This broken jaw of our lost kingdoms

In this last of meeting places
We grope together
And avoid speech
Gathered on this beach of the tumid river   60

Sightless, unless
The eyes reappear
As the perpetual star
Multifoliate rose
Of death's twilight kingdom
The hope only
Of empty men.

V

Here we go round the prickly pear
Prickly pear prickly pear
Here we go round the prickly pear   70
At five o'clock in the morning.

Between the idea
And the reality
Between the motion

And the act
Falls the Shadow

For Thine is the Kingdom

Between the conception
And the creation
Between the emotion   80
And the response
Falls the Shadow

Life is very long

Between the desire
And the spasm
Between the potency
And the existence
Between the essence
And the descent
Falls the Shadow   90

For Thine is the Kingdom

For Thine is
Life is
For Thine is the

This is the way the world ends
This is the way the world ends
This is the way the world ends
Not with a bang but a whimper.

T. S. Eliot

The chief use of the "meaning" of a poem in the ordinary sense, may be . . . to satisfy one habit of the reader, to keep his mind diverted and quiet, while the poem does its work upon him.

T. S. Eliot

To Margaret

Spring and Fall

Margaret, are you grieving
Over Goldengrove unleaving?
Leaves, like the things of man, you
With your fresh thoughts care for, can you?
Ah! as the heart grows older
It will come to such sights colder
By and by, nor spare a sigh
Though worlds of wanwood leafmeal lie;
And yet you will weep and know why.
Now no matter, child, the name:
Sorrow's springs are the same.
Nor mouth had, no nor mind, expressed
What heart heard of, ghost guessed:
It is the blight man was born for,
It is Margaret you mourn for.

Gerard Manley Hopkins

The Windhover

To Christ our Lord

I caught this morning morning's minion, king-
   dom of daylight's dauphin, dapple-dawn-drawn Falcon, in his riding
   Of the rolling level underneath him steady air, and striding
High there, how he rung upon the rein of a wimpling wing
In his ecstasy! then off, off forth on swing,
   As a skate's heel sweeps smooth on a bow-bend: the hurl and gliding
   Rebuffed the big wind. My heart in hiding
Stirred for a bird,—the achieve of, the mastery of the thing!

Brute beauty and valour and act, oh, air, pride, plume here
   Buckle! AND the fire that breaks from thee then, a billion
   Times told lovelier, more dangerous, O my chevalier!

   No wonder of it: shéer plód makes plough down sillion
Shine, and blue-bleak embers, ah my dear,
   Fall, gall themselves, and gash gold-vermilion.

Gerard Manley Hopkins

The Carpenter's Son

"Here the hangman stops his cart:
Now the best of friends must part.
Fare you well, for ill fare I:
Live, lads, and I will die.

"Oh, at home had I but stayed
'Prenticed to my father's trade,
Had I stuck to plane and adze,
I had not been lost, my lads.

"Then I might have built perhaps
Gallow-trees for other chaps,
Never dangled on my own,
Had I but left ill alone.

"Now, you see, they hang me high,
And the people passing by
Stop to shake their fists and curse;
So 'tis come from ill to worse.

"Here hang I, and right and left
Two poor fellows hang for theft:
All the same's the luck we prove,
Though the midmost hangs for love.

"Comrades all, that stand and gaze,
Walk henceforth in other ways;
See my neck and save your own:
Comrades all, leave ill alone.

"Make some day a decent end,
Shrewder fellows than your friend.
Fare you well, for ill fare I:
Live, lads, and I will die."

A. E. Housman

Eight O'Clock

He stood, and heard the steeple
  Sprinkle the quarters on the morning town.
One, two, three, four, to market-place and people
  It tossed them down.

Strapped, noosed, nighing his hour,
  He stood and counted them and cursed his luck;
And then the clock collected in the tower
  Its strength, and struck.

A. E. Housman

To My Brothers

Small, busy flames play through the fresh laid coals,
 And their faint cracklings o'er our silence creep
 Like whispers of the household gods that keep
A gentle empire o'er fraternal souls.
And while, for rhymes, I search around the poles,
 Your eyes are fix'd, as in poetic sleep,
 Upon the lore so voluble and deep,
That aye at fall of night our care condoles.
This is your birth-day Tom, and I rejoice
 That thus it passes smoothly, quietly.
Many such eves of gently whisp'ring noise
 May we together pass, and calmly try
What are this world's true joys,—ere the great voice,
 From its fair face, shall bid our spirits fly.

John Keats

When I have fears that I may cease to be
Before my pen has glean'd my teeming brain,
Before high pilèd books, in charact'ry,
Hold like rich garners the full-ripen'd grain;
When I behold, upon the night's starr'd face,
Huge cloudy symbols of a high romance,
And think that I may never live to trace
Their shadows, with the magic hand of chance;
And when I feel, fair creature of an hour!
That I shall never look upon thee more,
Never have relish in the faery power
Of unreflecting love!—then on the shore
 Of the wide world I stand alone, and think
 Till Love and Fame to nothingness do sink.

John Keats

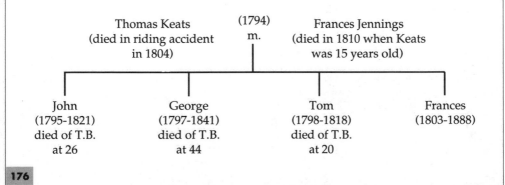

Thomas Keats
(died in riding accident
in 1804)

(1794)
m.

Frances Jennings
(died in 1810 when Keats
was 15 years old)

John
(1795-1821)
died of T.B.
at 26

George
(1797-1841)
died of T.B.
at 44

Tom
(1798-1818)
died of T.B.
at 20

Frances
(1803-1888)

Madonna of the Evening Flowers

All day I have been working,
Now I am tired.
I call: "Where are you?"
But there is only the oak tree rustling in the wind.
The house is very quiet,
The sun shines in on your books,
On your scissors and thimble just put down,
But you are not there.
Suddenly I am lonely:
Where are you?   10
I go about searching.
Then I see you,
Standing under a spire of pale blue larkspur,
With a basket of roses on your arm.
You are cool, like silver,
And you smile.

I think the Canterbury bells are playing little tunes,
You tell me that the peonies need spraying,
That the columbines have overrun all bounds,
That the pyrus japonica should be cut back and
        rounded.   20
You tell me these things.
But I look at you, heart of silver,
White heart-flame of polished silver,
Burning beneath the blue steeples of the larkspur,
And I long to kneel instantly at your feet,
While all about us peal the loud, sweet *Te Deums* of the
        Canterbury bells.

Amy Lowell

Opal

You are ice and fire,
The touch of you burns my hands like snow.
You are cold and flame.
You are the crimson of amaryllis,
The silver of moon-touched magnolias.
When I am with you,
My heart is a frozen pond
Gleaming with agitated torches.

Amy Lowell

Sonnet 29

When in disgrace with fortune and men's eyes
I all alone beweep my outcast state,
And trouble deaf heaven with my bootless cries,
And look upon myself and curse my fate,
Wishing me like to one more rich in hope,
Featured like him, like him with friends possessed,
Desiring this man's art, and that man's scope,
With what I most enjoy contented least;
Yet in these thoughts myself almost despising,
Haply I think on thee—and then my state,
Like to the lark at break of day arising
From sullen earth, sings hymns at heaven's gate;
    For thy sweet love remembered, such wealth brings
    That then I scorn to change my state with kings.

William Shakespeare

from The Merchant of Venice

(IV:1:195-208)

The quality of mercy is not strained;
It droppeth as the gentle rain from heaven
Upon the place beneath. It is twice blest;
It blesseth him that gives and him that takes.
'Tis mightiest in the mightiest; it becomes
The thronèd monarch better than his crown.
His sceptre shows the force of temporal power,
The attribute to awe and majesty,
Wherein doth sit the dread and fear of kings;
But mercy is above this scept'red sway;
It is enthronèd in the hearts of kings;
It is an attribute to God himself,
And earthly power doth then show likest God's
When mercy seasons justice.

William Shakespeare

Many wearing rapiers are afraid of goosequills.

Hamlet (I:2:308)

from **A**s You Like It

(II:7:138-165)

>   All the world's a stage,
> And all the men and women merely players;
> They have their exits and their entrances,
> And one man in his time plays many parts,
> His acts being seven ages. At first the infant,
> Mewling and puking in the nurse's arms.
> Then the whining schoolboy, with his satchel
> And shining morning face, creeping like snail
> Unwillingly to school. And then the lover,
> Sighing like furnace, with a woeful ballad   10
> Made to his mistress' eyebrow. Then a soldier,
> Full of strange oaths, and bearded like the pard,
> Jealous in honour, sudden, and quick in quarrel,
> Seeking the bubble reputation
> Even in the cannon's mouth. And then the justice,
> In fair round belly with good capon lin'd,
> With eyes severe and beard of formal cut,
> Full of wise saws and modern instances;
> And so he plays his part. The sixth age shifts
> Into the lean and slipper'd pantaloon,   20
> With spectacles on nose, and pouch on side,
> His youthful hose, well sav'd, a world too wide
> For his shrunk shank, and his big manly voice,
> Turning again toward childish treble, pipes
> And whistles in his sound. Last scene of all,
> That ends this strange eventful history,
> Is second childishness, and mere oblivion,
> Sans teeth, sans eyes, sans taste, sans every thing.

from **M**acbeth   *William Shakespeare*

(V:5:19-28)

To-morrow, and to-morrow, and to-morrow,
Creeps in this petty pace from day to day,
To the last syllable of recorded time;
And all our yesterdays, have lighted fools
The way to dusty death. Out, out, brief candle,
Life's but a walking shadow, a poor player
That struts and frets his hour upon the stage,
And then is heard no more. It is a tale
Told by an idiot, full of sound and fury,
Signifying nothing.

William Shakespeare

from Song of Myself

1

I celebrate myself, and sing myself,
And what I assume you shall assume,
For every atom belonging to me as good belongs to you.

I loafe and invite my soul,
I lean and loafe at my ease observing a spear of summer
    grass.

My tongue, every atom of my blood, form'd from this soil,
    this air,
Born here of parents born here from parents the same, and
    their parents the same,
I, now thirty-seven years old in perfect health begin,
Hoping to cease not till death.

Creeds and schools in abeyance,   10
Retiring back a while sufficed at what they are, but never
    forgotten,
I harbour for good or bad, I permit to speak at every hazard,
Nature without check with original energy.

6

A child said *What is the grass?* fetching it to me with full
    hands;
How could I answer the child? I do not know what it is
    any more than he.

I guess it must be the flag of my disposition, out of hopeful
    green stuff woven.

Or I guess it is the handkerchief of the Lord,
A scented gift and remembrancer designedly dropt,
Bearing the owner's name someway in the corners, that we
    may see and remark, and say *Whose?*

Or I guess the grass is itself a child, the produced babe of
    the vegetation.   20

Or I guess it is a uniform hieroglyphic,
And it means, Sprouting alike in broad zones and narrow
    zones,
Growing among black folks as among white,
Kanuck, Tuckahoe, Congressman, Cuff, I give them the
    same, I receive them the same.

And now it seems to me the beautiful uncut hair of graves.

Walt Whitman

A Slumber Did My Spirit Seal

A slumber did my spirit seal;
  I had no human fears:
She seem'd a thing that could not feel
  The touch of earthly years.

No motion has she now, no force;
  She neither hears nor sees;
Roll'd round in earth's diurnal course
  With rocks, and stones, and trees.

William Wordsworth

My Heart Leaps Up When I Behold

My heart leaps up when I behold
  A rainbow in the sky;
So was it when my life began;
So is it now I am a man;
So be it when I shall grow old.
  Or let me die!
The Child is father of the Man;
And I could wish my days to be
Bound each to each by natural piety.

William Wordsworth

The World Is too Much with Us

The world is too much with us; late and soon,
Getting and spending, we lay waste our powers:
Little we see in Nature that is ours;
We have given our hearts away, a sordid boon!
The Sea that bares her bosom to the moon;
The winds that will be howling at all hours,
And are up-gathered now like sleeping flowers;
For this, for everything, we are out of tune;
It moves us not.—Great God! I'd rather be
A Pagan suckled in a creed outworn;
So might I, standing on this pleasant lea,
Have glimpses that would make me less forlorn;
Have sight of Proteus rising from the sea;
Or hear old Triton blow his wreathèd horn.

William Wordsworth

Sailing to Byzantium

That is no country for old men. The young
In one another's arms, birds in the trees
—Those dying generations—at their song,
The salmon-falls, the mackerel-crowded seas,
Fish, flesh, or fowl, commend all summer long
Whatever is begotten, born, and dies.
Caught in that sensual music all neglect
Monuments of unaging intellect.

An aged man is but a paltry thing,
A tattered coat upon a stick, unless
Soul clap its hands and sing, and louder sing
For every tatter in its mortal dress,
Nor is there singing school but studying
Monuments of its own magnificence;
And therefore I have sailed the seas and come
To the holy city of Byzantium.

O sages standing in God's holy fire
As in the gold mosaic of a wall,
Come from the holy fire, perne in a gyre,
And be the singing-masters of my soul.
Consume my heart away; sick with desire
And fastened to a dying animal
It knows not what it is; and gather me
Into the artifice of eternity.

Once out of nature I shall never take
My bodily form from any natural thing,
But such a form as Grecian goldsmiths make
Of hammered gold and gold enameling
To keep a drowsy Emperor awake;
Or set upon a golden bough to sing
To lords and ladies of Byzantium
Of what is past, or passing, or to come.

William Butler Yeats

Blood, imagination, and intellect.

William Butler Yeats

On Being Asked for a War Poem

I think it better that in times like these
A poet's mouth be silent, for in truth
We have no gift to set a statesman right;
He has had enough of meddling who can please
A young girl in the indolence of her youth,
Or an old man upon a winter's night.

William Butler Yeats

When You Are Old

When you are old and grey and full of sleep,
And nodding by the fire, take down this book,
And slowly read, and dream of the soft look
Your eyes had once, and of their shadows deep;

How many loved your moments of glad grace,
And loved your beauty with love false or true;
But one man loved the pilgrim soul in you,
And loved the sorrows of your changing face.

And bending down beside the glowing bars
Murmur, a little sadly, how love fled
And paced upon the mountains overhead
And hid his face amid a crowd of stars.

William Butler Yeats

The Lake Isle of Innisfree

I will arise and go now, and go to Innisfree,
And a small cabin build there, of clay and wattles made;
Nine bean rows will I have there, a hive for the honey bee,
    And live alone in the bee-loud glade.

And I shall have some peace there, for peace comes dropping slow,
Dropping from the veils of the morning to where the cricket sings;
There midnight's all a glimmer, and noon a purple glow,
    And evening full of the linnet's wings.

I will arise and go now, for always night and day
I hear lake water lapping with low sounds by the shore;
While I stand on the roadway, or on the pavements grey,
    I hear it in the deep heart's core.

William Butler Yeats

• • DISC POETRY = songs that have poetic merit that one hears on the
radio airwaves or on CDs, cassettes, and records.

•• **E**lectric poetry of the airwaves.

Morning Has Broken

Morning has broken like the first morning,
Black bird has spoken like the first bird.
Praise for the singing! Praise for the morning!
Praise for them springing fresh from the word.

Sweet the rain's new fall, sunlit from heaven,
Like the first dewfall on the first grass.
Praise for the sweetness of the wet garden,
Sprung in completeness where his feet pass.

Mine is the sunlight! Mine is the morning
Born of the one light Eden saw play.
Praise with elation, praise every morning,
God's recreation of the new day.

Eleanor Farjeon

*Poetry is art and does what art can do — trap
heaven and earth in the cage of form.*

Archibald MacLeish

Delight is the chief, if not the only, end of poetry.

John Dryden

Big Yellow Taxi

They paved paradise
Put up a parkin' lot
With a pink hotel, a boutique
And a swingin' hot spot
Don't it always seem to go
That you don't know what you've got
Till it's gone
They paved paradise
Put up a parkin' lot.

They took all the trees
Put them in a tree museum
And they charged the people
A dollar and a half just to see 'em
Don't it always seem to go
That you don't know what you've got
Till it's gone
They paved paradise
Put up a parkin' lot.

Hey farmer farmer
Put away that D.D.T. now
Give me spots on my apples
But leave me the birds and the bees
Please!
Don't it always seem to go
That you don't know what you've got
Till it's gone
They paved paradise
Put up a parkin' lot.

Late last night
I heard the screen door slam
And a big yellow taxi
Took away my old man
Don't it always seem to go
That you don't know what you've got
Till it's gone
They paved paradise
Put up a parkin' lot
I said, don't it always seem to go
That you don't know what you've got
Till it's gone
They paved paradise
Put up a parkin' lot…

Joni Mitchell

One Tin Soldier

Listen children to a story that was written long ago
'Bout a kingdom on a mountain, and the valley folk below.
On the mountain was a treasure buried deep beneath a stone,
And the valley people swore they'd have it for their very own.

> Go ahead and hate your neighbour,
> Go ahead and cheat a friend.
> Do it in the name of heaven.
> Justify it in the end.
> There won't be any trumpets blowin'
> Come the judgement day,
> On the bloody morning after…
> One tin soldier rides away.

So the people of the valley sent a message up the hill,
Asking for the buried treasure, tons of gold for which they'd kill.
Came the answer from the kingdom, "With our brothers we will share
All the secrets of our mountain, all the riches buried there."

Now the valley cried with anger, "Mount your horses, draw your sword,"
And they killed the mountain people, so they won their just reward.
Now they stood beside the treasure on the mountain, dark and red,
Turned the stone and looked beneath it, "Peace on earth" was all it said.

> Go ahead and hate your neighbour,
> Go ahead and cheat a friend.
> Do it in the name of heaven.
> Justify it in the end.
> There won't be any trumpets blowin'
> Come the judgement day,
> On the bloody morning after…
> One tin soldier rides away.

Dennis Lambert and Brian Potter

No surprise for the writer, no surprise for the reader. For me the initial delight is in the surprise of remembering something I didn't know I knew.

Robert Frost

Wondering Where the Lions Are

Sun's up, uh huh, looks okay
the world survives into another day
and i'm thinking about eternity
some kind of ecstasy got a hold on me.

I had another dream about lions at the door
they weren't half as frightening as they were before
but i'm thinking about eternity
some kind of ecstasy got a hold on me.

Walls windows trees, waves coming through
you be in me and i'll be in you
together in eternity
some kind of ecstasy got a hold on me.

Up among the firs where it smells so sweet
or down in the valley where the river used to be
i got my mind on eternity
some kind of ecstasy got a hold on me.
and i'm wondering where the lions are…
i'm wondering where the lions are…

Huge orange flying boat rises off a lake
thousand-year-old petroglyphs doing a double-take
pointing a finger at eternity
i'm sitting in the middle of this ecstasy.

Young men marching, helmets shining in the sun
polished and precise like the brain behind the gun
(should be) they got me thinking about eternity
some kind of ecstasy got a hold on me.
and i'm wondering where the lions are…
i'm wondering where the lions are…

Freighters on the nod on the surface of the bay
one of these days we're going to sail away
going to sail into eternity
some kind of ecstasy got a hold on me.
and i'm wondering where the lions are…
i'm wondering where the lions are…

Bruce Cockburn

World of Wonders

stand on a bridge before the cavern of night
darkness alive with possibility
nose to this wind full of twinkling lights
trying to catch the scent of what's coming to be
    (in this…)

       world of wonders…

somewhere a saxophone slides thru changes
like a wet pipe dripping down my neck
gives me a chill—sounds like danger
but i can't stop moving till i cross this sector
    (of this…)

       world of wonders…

there's a rainbow shining in a bead of spittle
falling diamonds in rattling rain
light flexed on moving muscle
i stand here dazzled with my heart in flames
    (at this…)

       world of wonders…

moment of peace like brief arctic bloom
red/gold ripple of the sun going down
line of black hills makes my bed
sky full of love pulled over my head
    (in this…)

       world of wonders…

Bruce Cockburn

The ideal reader must be sensitive to words over their whole poetic range, and respond to poetry musically, emotionally, imaginatively.

Katherine M. Wilson

The Boy in the Bubble

It was a slow day
And the sun was beating
On the soldiers by the side of the road
There was a bright light
A shattering of shop windows
The bomb in the baby carriage
Was wired to the radio

These are the days of miracle and wonder
This is the long distance call
The way the camera follows us in slo-mo
The way we look to us all
The way we look to a distant constellation
That's dying in a corner of the sky
These are the days of miracle and wonder
And don't cry baby, don't cry
Don't cry

It was a dry wind
And it swept across the desert
And it curled into the circle of birth
And the dead sand
Falling on the children
The mothers and the fathers
And the automatic earth

These are the days of miracle and wonder
This is the long distance call
The way the camera follows us in slo-mo
The way we look to us all
The way we look to a distant constellation
That's dying in a corner of the sky
These are the days of miracle and wonder
And don't cry baby, don't cry
Don't cry

It's a turn-around jump shot
It's everybody jump start
It's every generation throws a hero up the pop charts
Medicine is magical and magical is art
The Boy in the Bubble
And the baby with the baboon heart

And I believe
These are the days of lasers in the jungle
Lasers in the jungle somewhere
Staccato signals of constant information
A loose affiliation of millionaires
And billionaires and baby

These are the days of miracle and wonder
This is the long distance call
The way the camera follows us in slo-mo
The way we look to us all
The way we look to a distant constellation
That's dying in a corner of the sky
These are the days of miracle and wonder
And don't cry baby, don't cry
Don't cry

Paul Simon

I Am a Rock

A winter's day
In a deep and dark December—
I am alone
Gazing from my window
To the streets below
On a freshly fallen silent shroud of snow.
I am a rock;
I am an island.

I build walls,
A fortress deep and mighty
That none may penetrate.
I have no need of friendship;
Friendship causes pain.
Its laughter and its loving I disdain.
I am a rock;
I am an island.

Don't talk of love.
Well, I've heard the word before;
It's sleeping in my memory
I won't disturb the slumber
Of feelings that have died.
If I'd never loved, I never would have cried.
I am a rock;
I am an island.

I have my books
And my poetry to protect me.
I am shielded in my armour,
Hiding in my room
Safe within my tomb.
I touch no one and no one touches me.
I am a rock;
I am an island.

And a rock feels no pain,
And an island never cries.

Paul Simon

Scarborough Fair

Where are you going, to Scarborough Fair?
Savory, sage, rosemary, and thyme,
Remember me to a lass who lives there,
For once she was a true love of mine.

Tell her to make me a cambric shirt,
Savory, sage, rosemary, and thyme,
Without any sewing or needle work,
And then she shall be a true love of mine.

Tell her to wash it in yonder well,
Savory, sage, rosemary, and thyme,
Where no water flowed there nor drop of rain fell,
And then she shall be a true love of mine.

Tell her to hang it on yonder green thorn,
Savory, sage, rosemary, and thyme,
That never bore blossom since Adam was born,
And then she shall be a true love of mine.

Where are you going, to Scarborough Fair?
Savory, sage, rosemary, and thyme.
Remember me to a lad who lives there,
For he was once a true love of mine.

Tell him to make me an acre of land,
Savory, sage, rosemary, and thyme,
Between the sea foam and the sea sand,
Then he shall be a true love of mine.

Tell him to plow it all with a ram's horn,
Savory, sage, rosemary, and thyme,
And sow it all with one peppercorn,
And then he shall be a true love of mine.

Tell him to reap it with sickle of leather,
Savory, sage, rosemary, and thyme,
And thresh it all up with but one peacock feather,
And then he shall be a true love of mine.

traditional English ballad

Régine

Sister Régine was the pretty one
She never was lonely for long
And I was poor Ellen the plain one
Who never did anything wrong

Our mother died when we were both young
And I learned to cook and clean
Father died slowly of cancer and care
And always he talked of Régine

Régine walks like a queen
Loves like a child, lives in a dream
Régine what have you done
You took all the love and left me with none

Régine left the farm at seventeen
She had children by two different men
And as she bore them she brought them to me
And I was a mother to them

I was near thirty when I married Carl
And I know that he married the land
But he's steady and he's kind and he's good to the girls
And I know the place needed a man

My sister's two daughters are like night and day
And my heart is caught in between
For one of them's pretty and one of them's plain
And the pretty one looks like Régine

For sister Régine was the pretty one
Who carried herself like a queen
And I am poor Ellen the plain one
Who wishes that she were Régine

Sylvia Tyson

The Music of the Night

Night-time sharpens, heightens each sensation...
Darkness stirs and wakes imagination...
Silently the senses abandon their defences.

Slowly, gently, night unfurls its splendour;
Grasp it, sense it—tremulous and tender.
Turn your face away
From the garish light of day;
Turn your thoughts away
From cold, unfeeling light
And listen to the music of the night.

Close your eyes and surrender to your darkest dreams!
Purge your thoughts of the life in you before!
Close your eyes, let your spirit start to soar!
And you'll live as you've never lived before.

Softly, deftly, music shall surround you;
Feel it, hear it, closing in around you.
Open up your mind; let your fantasies unwind
In this darkness which you know you cannot fight—
The darkness of the music of the night.

Let your mind start a journey through a strange new world!
Leave all thoughts of the world you knew before!
Let your soul take you where you long to be!
Only then can you belong to me.

Floating, falling, sweet intoxication!
Touch me, trust me, savour each sensation!
Let the dream begin; let your darker side give in
To the power of the music that I write—
The power of the music of the night.

You alone can make my song take flight—
Help me make the music of the night.

Charles Hart

▣ Superman

O Superman. O Judge. O Mom and Dad. Mom and Dad.
Hi. I'm not home right now. But if you want to leave a
    message, just start talking at the sound of the tone.
Hello? This is your Mother. Are you there? Are you coming home?
Hello? Is anybody home? Well, you don't know me,
    but I know you.
And I've got a message to give to you.
    Here come the planes.
So you better get ready. Ready to go. You can come
    as you are, but pay as you go. Pay as you go.

And I said: OK. Who is this really? And the voice said:
This is the hand, the hand that takes. This is the
    hand, the hand that takes.
This is the hand, the hand that takes.
    Here come the planes.
They're American planes. Made in America.
Smoking or non-smoking?
And the voice said: Neither snow nor rain nor gloom
    of night shall stay these couriers from the swift
    completion of their appointed rounds.

'Cause when love is gone, there's always justice.
    And when justice is gone, there's always force.
    And when force is gone, there's always Mom. Hi Mom!

So hold me, Mom, in your long arms. So hold me,
    Mom, in your long arms.
In your automatic arms. Your electronic arms.
    In your arms.
So hold me, Mom, in your long arms.
Your petrochemical arms. Your military arms.
In your electronic arms.

Laurie Anderson

The poet's craft is to turn words into deeds.

Elizabeth Drew

Don't Give Up

in this proud land we grew up strong
we were wanted all along
I was taught to fight, taught to win
I never thought I could fail

no fight left or so it seems
I am a man whose dreams have all deserted
I've changed my face, I've changed my name
but no one wants you when you lose

don't give up
'cause you have friends
don't give up
you're not beaten yet
don't give up
I know you can make it good

though I saw it all around
never thought that I could be affected
thought that we'd be last to go
it is so strange the way things turn

drove the night toward my home
the place that I was born, on the lakeside
as daylight broke, I saw the earth
the trees had burned down to the ground

don't give up
you still have us
don't give up
we don't need much of anything
don't give up
'cause somewhere there's a place
where we belong

rest your head
you worry too much
it's going to be alright
when times get rough
you can fall back on us
don't give up
please don't give up

got to walk out of here
I can't take any more
going to stand on that bridge
keep my eyes down below
whatever may come
and whatever may go
that river's flowing
that river's flowing

moved on to another town
tried hard to settle down
for every job, so many men
so many men no one needs

don't give up
'cause you have friends
don't give up
you're not the only one
don't give up
no reason to be ashamed
don't give up
you still have us
don't give up now
we're proud of who you are
don't give up
you know its never been easy
don't give up
'cause I believe there's a place
there's a place where we belong

Peter Gabriel

■ Still Haven't Found What I'm Looking For

I have climbed the highest mountains
I have run through the fields
Only to be with you
Only to be with you

I have run I have crawled
I have scaled these city walls
Only to be with you
But I still haven't found
What I'm looking for
But I still haven't found
What I'm looking for

I have kissed honey lips
Felt the healing in her fingertips
It burned like fire
This burning desire
I have spoke with the tongue of angels
I have held the hand of the devil
It was warm in the night
I was cold as a stone
But I still haven't found
What I'm looking for
But I still haven't found
What I'm looking for

I believe in the Kingdom Come
Then all the colours will bleed into one
But yes I'm still running
You broke the bonds
You loosed the chains
You carried the cross
And my shame
And my shame
You know I believe it
But I still haven't found
What I'm looking for
But I still haven't found
What I'm looking for

Paul Hewson (Bono)

Reggae Sounds

Shock-black bubble-doun-beat bouncing
rock-wise tumble-doun sound music;
foot-drop find drum, blood story
bass history is a moving
            is a hurting black story.

Thunda from a bass drum sounding
lightning from a trumpet and a organ,
bass and rhythm and trumpet double-up,
team up with drums for a dep doun searching.

Rhythm of a tropical electrical storm
(cooled doun to the pace of the struggle),
flame-rhythm of historically yearning
flame-rhythm of the time of turning,
measuring the time for bombs and for burning.

Slow drop. make stop. move forward.
dig doun to the root of the pain;
shape it into violence for the people,
they will know what to do, they will do it.

Shock-black bubble-doun-beat bouncing
rock-wise tumble-doun sound music;
foot-drop find drum, blood story,
bass history is a moving
            is a hurting black story.

Linton Kwesi Johnson

The Vision

The Leader

I looked to the North, and I turned to the West,
For a sign, a light in the sky.
Oh the message is clear that the time is near
For a leader to come again.

A circle of stones on the head of a hill;
Tonight is where it will be.
In this desolate place, we all stand and wait
For the leader to come again; yes a leader will come again.

For it is written that a leader will be here.
And then a vision left me blinded by the light,
And it started right in front of my eyes…

The Vision

And I saw a burning chariot,
And the four horsemen of the apocalypse
Waiting on high.
And I heard the thunder rolling in,
And behold our leader on a pale horse riding in the sky;

And I saw this land a battlefield
With a hundred thousand men fighting hand to hand.
And I heard the sounds of victory,
And the rivers ran red with the blood of our enemies.

And I saw the fire from the sky.
I saw fire, and I saw paradise,
Fire from the sun, I saw fire.
And I saw alpha and omega.
Fire. I saw fire.
And I saw paradise.
Fire. I saw fire.

What about Me?

I am left in the night, trembling with fear.
I have seen to the future, and the future is here.
Our leader will bring victory, but our land is in flames.
And as the final sounds of battle disappear, I had to say,

What about me, and you, and the ones that we love.
What about me, and you, and the ones that we love.
Well what about us?

Chris De Burgh

Questioning a Poem

These questions will help you to reach the heart of a poem.

1. Who is speaking in the poem?
2. What is the tone of the poem? (tone = the poet's attitude to the topic and the reader)
3. To whom is the poet speaking?
4. What is the setting of the poem?
5. When does the poem take place?
6. What mood is evoked by the poem?
7. Does the point of view change during the poem?
8. How does the poem make me feel?
9. Do I like the poem? Why?
10. What is the poet attempting to say? What insight, truth, moment of observation emerges from the poem?

Progressive Insanities of a Pioneer

i

He stood, a point
on a sheet of green paper
proclaiming himself the centre,

with no walls, no borders
anywhere; the sky no height
above him, totally un-
enclosed
and shouted:

Let me out!

ii

He dug the soil in rows,   10
imposed himself with shovels
He asserted
into the furrows, I
am not random.

The ground
replied with aphorisms:

a tree-sprout, a nameless
weed, words
he couldn't understand.

iii

The house pitched   20
the plot staked
in the middle of nowhere.

At night the mind
inside, in the middle
of nowhere.

The idea of an animal
patters across the roof.

In the darkness the fields
defend themselves with fences
in vain: 30
      everything
      is getting in.

iv

By daylight he resisted.
He said, disgusted
with the swamp's clamourings and the outbursts
of rocks,
      This is not order
      but the absence
      of order.

He was wrong, the unanswering   40
forest implied:

      It was
      an ordered absence

v

For many years
he fished for a great vision,
dangling the hooks of sown
roots under the surface
of the shallow earth.

It was like
enticing whales with a bent   50
pin. Besides he thought

in that country
only the worms were biting.

vi

If he had known unstructured
space is a deluge
and stocked his log house-
boat with all the animals

even the wolves,

he might have floated.

But obstinate he   60
stated, The land is solid
and stamped,

watching his foot sink
down through stone
up to the knee.

vii

Things
refused to name themselves; refused
to let him name them.

The wolves hunted
outside.   70

On his beaches, his clearings,
by the surf of under-
growth breaking
at his feet, he foresaw
disintegration
    and in the end
through eyes
made ragged by his
effort, the tension
between subject and object,   80

the green
vision, the unnamed
whale invaded.

Margaret Atwood

I believe that poetry is the heart of the
language, the activity through which
language is renewed and kept alive.

Margaret Atwood

The writer is both an eye-witness and
an I-witness, the one to whom personal
experience happens and the one who
makes experience personal for others.

Margaret Atwood

David

I

David and I that summer cut trails on the Survey,
All week in the valley for wages, in air that was steeped
In the wail of mosquitoes, but over the sunalive weekends
We climbed, to get from the ruck of the camp, the surly

Poker, the wrangling, the snoring under the fetid
Tents, and because we had joy in our lengthening coltish
Muscles, and mountains for David were made to see over,
Stairs from the valleys and steps to the sun's retreats.

II

Our first was Mount Gleam. We hiked in the long afternoon
To a curling lake and lost the lure of the faceted   10
Cone in the swell of its sprawling shoulders. Past
The inlet we grilled our bacon, the strips festooned

On a poplar prong, in the hurrying slant of the sunset.
Then the two of us rolled in the blanket while round us the cold
Pines thrust at the stars. The dawn was a floating
Of mists till we reached to the slopes above timber, and won

To snow like fire in the sunlight. The peak was upthrust
Like a fist in a frozen ocean of rock that swirled
Into valleys the moon could be rolled in. Remotely unfurling
Eastward the alien prairie glittered. Down through the dusty   20

Skree on the west we descended, and David showed me
How to use the give of shale for giant incredible
Strides. I remember, before the larches' edge,
That I jumped a long green surf of juniper flowing

Away from the wind, and landed in gentian and saxifrage
Spilled on the moss. Then the darkening firs
And the sudden whirring of water that knifed down a fern-hidden
Cliff and splashed unseen into mist in the shadows.

III

One Sunday on Rampart's arête a rainsquall caught us,
And passed, and we clung by our blueing fingers and bootnails   30
An endless hour in the sun, not daring to move
Till the ice had steamed from the slate. And David taught me

How time on a knife-edge can pass with the guessing of fragments
Remembered from poets, the naming of strata beside one,
And matching of stories from schooldays....We crawled astride
The peak to feast on the marching ranges flagged

By the fading shreds of the shattered stormcloud. Lingering
There it was David who spied to the south, remote,
And unmapped, a sunlit spire on Sawback, an overhang
Crooked like a talon. David named it the Finger.   40

That day we chanced on the skull and the splayed white ribs
Of a mountain goat underneath a cliff, caught
On a rock. Around were the silken feathers of hawks.
And that was the first I knew that a goat could slip.

IV

And then Inglismaldie. Now I remember only
The long ascent of the lonely valley, the live
Pine spirally scarred by lightning, the slicing pipe
Of invisible pika, and great prints, by the lowest

Snow, of a grizzly. There it was too that David
Taught me to read the scroll of coral in limestone   50
And the beetle-seal in the shale of ghostly trilobites,
Letters delivered to man from the Cambrian waves.

V

On Sundance we tried from the col and the going was hard.
The air howled from our feet to the smudged rocks
And the papery lake below. At an outthrust we balked
Till David clung with his left to a dint in the scarp,

Lobbed the iceaxe over the rocky lip,
Slipped from his holds and hung by the quivering pick,
Twisted his long legs up into space and kicked
To the crest. Then grinning, he reached with his freckled wrist   60

And drew me up after. We set a new time for that climb.
That day returning we found a robin gyrating
In grass, wing-broken. I caught it to tame but David
Took and killed it, and said, "Could you teach it to fly?"

VI

In August, the second attempt, we ascended The Fortress.
By the forks of the Spray we caught five trout and fried them
Over a balsam fire. The woods were alive
With the vaulting of mule-deer and drenched with clouds all
    the morning,

Till we burst at noon to the flashing and floating round
Of the peaks. Coming down we picked in our hats the bright   70
And sunhot raspberries, eating them under a mighty
Spruce, while a marten moving like quicksilver scouted us.

VII

But always we talked of the Finger on Sawback, unknown
And hooked, till the first afternoon in September we slogged
Through the musky woods, past a swamp that quivered with
    frog-song,
And camped by a bottle-green lake. But under the cold

Breath of the glacier sleep would not come, the moonlight
Etching the Finger. We rose and trod past the feathery
Larch, while the stars went out, and the quiet heather
Flushed, and the skyline pulsed with the surging bloom   80

Of incredible dawn in the Rockies. David spotted
Bighorns across the moraine and sent them leaping
With yodels the ramparts redoubled and rolled to the peaks
And the peaks to the sun. The ice in the morning thaw

Was a gurgling world of crystal and cold blue chasms,
And seracs that shone like frozen saltgreen waves.
At the base of the Finger we tried once and failed. Then David
Edged to the west and discovered the chimney; the last

Hundred feet we fought the rock and shouldered and kneed
Our way for an hour and made it. Unroping we formed   90
A cairn on the rotting tip. Then I turned to look north
At the glistening wedge of giant Assiniboine, heedless

Of handhold. And one foot gave. I swayed and shouted.
David turned sharp and reached out his arm and steadied me,
Turning again with a grin and his lips ready
To jest. But the strain crumbled his foothold. Without

A gasp he was gone. I froze to the sound of grating
Edge-nails and fingers, the slither of stones, the lone
Second of silence, the nightmare thud. Then only
The wind and the muted beat of unknowing cascades.   100

VIII

Somehow I worked down the fifty impossible feet
To the ledge, calling and getting no answer but echoes
Released in the cirque, and trying not to reflect
What an answer would mean. He lay still, with his lean

Young face upturned and strangely unmarred, but his legs
Splayed beneath him, beside the final drop,
Six hundred feet sheer to the ice. My throat stopped
When I reached him, for he was alive. He opened his grey

Straight eyes and brokenly murmured, "over...over."
And I, feeling beneath him a cruel fang   110
Of the ledge thrust in his back, but not understanding,
Mumbled stupidly, "Best not to move," and spoke

Of his pain. But he said, "I can't move...If only I felt
Some pain." Then my shame stung the tears to my eyes
As I crouched, and I cursed myself, but he cried,
Louder, "No, Bobbie! Don't ever blame yourself.

I didn't test my foothold." He shut the lids
Of his eyes to the stare of the sky, while I moistened his lips
From our water flask and tearing my shirt into strips
I swabbed the shredded hands. But the blood slid   120

From his side and stained the stone and the thirsting lichens,
And yet I dared not lift him up from the gore
Of the rock. Then he whispered, "Bob, I want to go over!"
This time I knew what he meant and I grasped for a lie

And said, "I'll be back here by midnight with ropes
And men from the camp and we'll cradle you out." But I knew
That the day and the night must pass and the cold dews
Of another morning before such men unknowing

The ways of mountains could win to the chimney's top.
And then, how long? And he knew...and the hell of hours   130
After that, if he lived till we came, roping him out.
But I curled beside him and whispered, "The bleeding will stop.

You can last." He said only, "Perhaps....For what? A wheelchair,
Bob?" His eyes brightening with fever upbraided me.
I could not look at him more and said, "Then I'll stay
With you." But he did not speak, for the clouding fever.

I lay dazed and stared at the long valley,
The glistening hair of a creek on the rug stretched
By the firs, while the sun leaned round and flooded the ledge,
The moss, and David still as a broken doll.   140

I hunched to my knees to leave, but he called and his voice
Now was sharpened with fear. "For Christ's sake push me over!
If I could move...Or die..." The sweat ran from his forehead,
But only his eyes moved. A hawk was buoying

Blackly its wings over the wrinkled ice.
The purr of a waterfall rose and sank with the wind.
Above us climbed the last joint of the Finger
Beckoning bleakly the wide indifferent sky.

Even then in the sun it grew cold lying there....And I knew
He had tested his holds. It was I who had not....I looked   150
At the blood on the ledge, and the far valley. I looked
At last in his eyes. He breathed, "I'd do it for you, Bob."

IX

I will not remember how nor why I could twist
Up the wind-devilled peak, and down through the chimney's
    empty
Horror, and over the traverse alone. I remember
Only the pounding fear I would stumble on It

When I came to the grave-cold maw of the bergschrund...reeling
Over the sun-cankered snowbridge, shying the caves
In the nêvé...the fear, and the need to make sure It was there
On the ice, the running and falling and running, leaping   160

Of gaping greenthroated crevasses, alone and pursued
By the Finger's lengthening shadow. At last through the fanged
And blinding seracs I slid to the milky wrangling
Falls at the glacier's snout, through the rocks piled huge

On the humped moraine, and into the spectral larches,
Alone. By the glooming lake I sank and chilled
My mouth but I could not rest and stumbled still
To the valley, losing my way in the ragged marsh.

I was glad of the mire that covered the stains, on my ripped
Boots, of his blood, but panic was on me, the reek   170
Of the bog, the purple glimmer of toadstools obscene
In the twilight. I staggered clear to a firewaste, tripped

And fell with a shriek on my shoulder. It somehow eased
My heart to know I was hurt, but I did not faint
And I could not stop while over me hung the range
Of the Sawback. In blackness I searched for the trail by the creek

And found it...My feet squelched a slug and horror
Rose again in my nostrils. I hurled myself
Down the path. In the woods behind some animal yelped.
Then I saw the glimmer of tents and babbled my story.   180

I said that he fell straight to the ice where they found him.
And none but the sun and incurious clouds have lingered
Around the marks of that day on the ledge of the Finger,
That day, the last of my youth, on the last of our mountains.

Earle Birney

The Love Song of J. Alfred Prufrock

S'io credesse che mia risposta fosse
A persona che mai tornasse al mondo,
Questa fiamma staria senza piu scosse.
Ma perciocche giammai di questo fondo
Non torno vivo alcun, s'i'odo il vero,
Senza tema d'infamia ti rispondo.

Let us go then, you and I,
When the evening is spread out against the sky
Like a patient etherized upon a table;
Let us go, through certain half-deserted streets,
The muttering retreats
Of restless nights in one-night cheap hotels
And sawdust restaurants with oyster-shells:
Streets that follow like a tedious argument
Of insidious intent
To lead you to an overwhelming question....   10
Oh, do not ask, "What is it?"
Let us go and make out visit.

In the room the women come and go
Talking of Michelangelo.

The yellow fog that rubs its back upon the window-panes,
The yellow smoke that rubs its muzzle on the window-panes
Licked its tongue into the corners of the evening,
Lingered upon the pools that stand in drains,
Let fall upon its back the soot that falls from chimneys,
Slipped by the terrace, made a sudden leap,   20
And seeing that it was a soft October night,
Curled once about the house, and fell asleep.

And indeed there will be time
For the yellow smoke that slides along the street
Rubbing its back upon the window-panes;
There will be time, there will be time
To prepare a face to meet the faces that you meet;
There will be time to murder and create,
And time for all the works and days of hands
That lift and drop a question on your plate;   30
Time for you and time for me,
And time yet for a hundred indecisions,
And for a hundred visions and revisions,
Before the taking of a toast and tea.

In the room the women come and go
Talking of Michelangelo.

And indeed there will be time
To wonder, "Do I dare?" and, "Do I dare?"
Time to turn back and descend the stair,
With a bald spot in the middle of my hair—   40
(They will say: "How his hair is growing thin!")
My morning coat, my collar mounting firmly to the chin,
My necktie rich and modest, but asserted by a simple pin—
(They will say: "But how his arms and legs are thin!")
Do I dare
Disturb the universe?
In a minute there is time
For decisions and revisions which a minute will reverse.

For I have known them all already, known them all —
Have known the evenings, mornings, afternoons,   50
I have measured out my life with coffee spoons;
I know the voices dying with a dying fall
Beneath the music from a farther room.
        So how should I presume?

And I have known the eyes already, known them all—
The eyes that fix you in a formulated phrase,
And when I am formulated, sprawling on a pin,
When I am pinned and wriggling on the wall,
Then how should I begin
To spit out all the butt-ends of my days and ways?   60
And how should I presume?

And I have known the arms already, known them all —
Arms that are braceleted and white and bare
(But in the lamplight, downed with light brown hair!)
Is it perfume from a dress
That makes me so digress?
Arms that lie along a table, or wrap about a shawl.
        And should I then presume?
        And how should I begin?

                    · · · · ·

Shall I say, I have gone at dusk through narrow streets   70
And watched the smoke that rises from the pipes
Of lonely men in shirt-sleeves, leaning out of windows?...

I should have been a pair of ragged claws
Scuttling across the floors of silent seas.

                    · · · · ·

And the afternoon, the evening, sleeps so peacefully!
Smoothed by long fingers,
Asleep…tired…or it malingers,
Stretched on the floor, here beside you and me.
Should I, after tea and cakes and ices,
Have the strength to force the moment to its crisis?　　　　　80
But though I have wept and fasted, wept and prayed,
Though I have seen my head (grown slightly bald) brought in
　　　upon a platter,
I am no prophet—and here's no great matter;
I have seen the moment of my greatness flicker,
And I have seen the eternal Footman hold my coat, and snicker,
And in short, I was afraid.

And would it have been worth it, after all,
After the cups, the marmalade, the tea,
Among the porcelain, among some talk of you and me,
Would it have been worth while,　　　　　90
To have bitten off the matter with a smile,
To have squeezed the universe into a ball
To roll it toward some overwhelming question,
To say: "I am Lazarus, come from the dead,
Come back to tell you all, I shall tell you all"—
If one, settling a pillow by her head,
　　　Should say: "That is not what I meant at all;
　　　That is not it, at all."

And would it have been worth it, after all,
Would it have been worth while,　　　　　100
After the sunsets and the dooryards and the sprinkled streets,
After the novels, after the teacups, after the skirts that trail
　　　along the floor—
And this, and so much more?—
It is impossible to say just what I mean!
But as if a magic lantern threw the nerves in patterns on a screen:
Would it have been worth while
If one, settling a pillow or throwing off a shawl,
And turning toward the window, should say:
　　　"That is not it at all,
　　　That is not what I meant, at all."　　　　　110

· · · · ·

No! I am not Prince Hamlet, nor was meant to be;
Am an attendant lord, one that will do
To swell a progress, start a scene or two,
Advise the prince; no doubt, an easy tool,
Deferential, glad to be of use,
Politic, cautious, and meticulous:
Full of high sentence, but a bit obtuse;
At times, indeed, almost ridiculous—
Almost, at times, the Fool.

I grow old....I grow old....   120
I shall wear the bottoms of my trousers rolled.

Shall I part my hair behind? Do I dare to eat a peach?
I shall wear white flannel trousers, and walk upon the beach.
I have heard the mermaids singing, each to each.

I do not think that they will sing to me.

I have seen them riding seaward on the waves
Combing the white hair of the waves blown back
When the wind blows the water white and black.

We have lingered in the chambers of the sea
By sea girls wreathed with seaweed red and brown   130
Till human voices wake us, and we drown.

T. S. Eliot

Poetry is the language of a state of crisis.

Stephane Malarmé

*I have tried to point out the importance of
the relation of the poem to other poems
by other authors, and suggested the
conception of poetry as a living whole of
all the poetry that has ever been written.*

T. S. Eliot

The Witch of Coös

I stayed the night for shelter at a farm
Behind the mountain, with a mother and son,
Two old-believers. They did all the talking.

MOTHER. Folks think a witch who has familiar spirits
She could call up to pass a winter evening,
But won't, should be burned at the stake or something.
Summoning spirits isn't 'Button, button,
Who's got the button,' I would have them know.

SON. Mother can make a common table rear
And kick with two legs like an army mule.   10

MOTHER. And when I've done it, what good have I done?
Rather than tip a table for you, let me
Tell you what Ralle the Sioux Control once told me.
He said the dead had souls, but when I asked him
How could that be—I thought the dead were souls,
He broke my trance. Don't that make you suspicious
That there's something the dead are keeping back?
Yes, there's something the dead are keeping back.

SON. You wouldn't want to tell him what we have
Up attic, mother?

MOTHER. Bones—a skeleton.   20

SON. But the headboard of mother's bed is pushed
Against the attic door: the door is nailed.
It's harmless. Mother hears it in the night
Halting perplexed behind the barrier
Of door and headboard. Where it wants to get
Is back into the cellar where it came from.

MOTHER. We'll never let them, will we, son! We'll never!

SON. It left the cellar forty years ago
And carried itself like a pile of dishes
Up one flight from the cellar to the kitchen,   30
Another from the kitchen to the bedroom,
Another from the bedroom to the attic,
Right past both father and mother, and neither stopped it.
Father had gone upstairs; mother was downstairs.
I was a baby: I don't know where I was.

MOTHER. The only fault my husband found with me—
I went to sleep before I went to bed,
Especially in winter when the bed
Might just as well be ice and the clothes snow.

The night the bones came up the cellar-stairs   40
Toffile had gone to bed alone and left me,
But left an open door to cool the room off
So as to sort of turn me out of it.
I was just coming to myself enough
To wonder where the cold was coming from,
When I heard Toffile upstairs in the bedroom
And thought I heard him downstairs in the cellar.
The board we had laid down to walk dry-shod on
When there was water in the cellar in spring
Struck the hard cellar bottom. And then someone   50
Began the stairs, two footsteps for each step,
The way a man with one leg and a crutch,
Or a little child, comes up. It wasn't Toffile:
It wasn't anyone who could be there.
The bulkhead double-doors were double-locked
And swollen tight and buried under snow.
The cellar windows were banked up with sawdust
And swollen tight and buried under snow.
It was the bones. I knew them—and good reason.
My first impulse was to get to the knob   60
And hold the door. But the bones didn't try
The door; they halted helpless on the landing,
Waiting for things to happen in their favour.
The faintest restless rustling ran all through them.
I never could have done the thing I did
If the wish hadn't been too strong in me
To see how they were mounted for this walk.
I had a vision of them put together
Not like a man, but like a chandelier.
So suddenly I flung the door wide on him.   70
A moment he stood balancing with emotion,
And all but lost himself. (A tongue of fire
Flashed out and licked along his upper teeth.
Smoke rolled inside the sockets of his eyes.)
Then he came at me with one hand outstretched,
The way he did in life once; but this time
I struck the hand off brittle on the floor,
And fell back from him on the floor myself.
The finger-pieces slid in all directions.
(Where did I see one of those pieces lately?   80
Hand me my button-box—it must be there.)
I sat up on the floor and shouted, 'Toffile,
It's coming up to you.' It had its choice
Of the door to the cellar or the hall.
It took the hall door for the novelty,

And set off briskly for so slow a thing,
Still going every which way in the joints, though,
So that it looked like lightning or a scribble,
From the slap I had just now given its hand.
I listened till it almost climbed the stairs   90
From the hall to the only finished bedroom,
Before I got up to do anything;
Then ran and shouted, 'Shut the bedroom door,
Toffile, for my sake!' 'Company?' he said,
'Don't make me get up; I'm too warm in bed.'
So lying forward weakly on the handrail
I pushed myself upstairs, and in the light
(The kitchen had been dark) I had to own
I could see nothing. 'Toffile, I don't see it.
It's with us in the room though. It's the bones.'   100
'What bones?' 'The cellar bones—out of the grave.'
That made him throw his bare legs out of bed
And sit up by me and take hold of me.
I wanted to put out the light and see
If I could see it, or else mow the room,
With our arms at the level of our knees,
And bring the chalk-pile down. 'I'll tell you what—
It's looking for another door to try.
The uncommonly deep snow has made him think
Of his old song, *The Wild Colonial Boy*,   110
He always used to sing along the tote road.
'He's after an open door to get outdoors.
Let's trap him with an open door up attic.'
Toffile agreed to that, and sure enough,
Almost the moment he was given an opening,
The steps began to climb the attic stairs.
I heard them. Toffile didn't seem to hear them.
'Quick!' I slammed to the door and held the knob.
'Toffile, get nails.' I made him nail the door shut
And push the headboard of the bed against it.   120
Then we asked was there anything
Up attic that we'd ever want again.
The attic was less to us than the cellar.
If the bones liked the attic, let them have it.
Let them stay in the attic. When they sometimes
Come down the stairs at night and stand perplexed
Behind the door and headboard of the bed,
Brushing their chalky skull with chalky fingers,
With sounds like the dry rattling of a shutter,
That's what I sit up in the dark to say—   130
To no one any more since Toffile died.

Let them stay in the attic since they went there.
I promised Toffile to be cruel to them
For helping them be cruel once to him.

SON. We think they had a grave down in the cellar.

MOTHER. We know they had a grave down in the cellar.

SON. We never could find out whose bones they were.

MOTHER. Yes, we could too, son. Tell the truth for once.
They were a man's his father killed for me.
I mean a man he killed instead of me.   140
The least I could do was to help dig their grave.
We were about it one night in the cellar.
Son knows the story: but 'twas not for him
To tell the truth, suppose the time had come.
Son looks surprised to see me end a lie
We'd kept all these years between ourselves
So as to have it ready for outsiders.
But tonight I don't care enough to lie—
I don't remember why I ever cared.
Toffile, if he were here, I don't believe   150
Could tell you why he ever cared himself....

She hadn't found the finger-bone she wanted
Among the buttons poured out in her lap.
I verified the name next morning: Toffile.
The rural letter box said Toffile Lajway.

Robert Frost

*There are two ways of coming close to poetry.
One is by writing poetry.*

*But as I say, there is another way to come close
to poetry, fortunately, and that is in the reading
of it, not as linguistics, not as history, not as
anything but poetry.*

Robert Frost

*Poetry is the imaginative expression of strong
feeling...the spontaneous overflow of powerful
feelings recollected in tranquillity.*

William Wordsworth

The Truth

When I was four my father went to Scotland.
They *said* he went to Scotland.

When I woke up I think I thought that I was dreaming—
I was so little then that I thought dreams
Are in the room with you, like the cinema.
That's why you don't dream when it's still light—
They pull the shades down when it is, so you can sleep.
I thought that then, but that's not right.
Really it's in your head.

And it was light then—light at *night*.   10
I heard Stalky bark outside.
But really it was Mother crying—
She coughed so hard she cried.
She kept shaking Sister,
She shook her and shook her.
I thought Sister had had her nightmare.
But he wasn't barking, he had died.
There was dirt all over Sister.
It was all streaks, like mud, I cried.
She didn't, but she was older.   20
                                        I thought she didn't
Because she was older, I thought Stalky had just gone.
I got *everything* wrong.
I didn't get one single thing right.
It seems to me that I'd have thought
It didn't happen, like a dream,
Except that it was light. At night.
They burnt our house down, they burnt down London.
Next day my mother cried all day, and after that
She said to me when she would come to see me:
"Your father has gone away to Scotland.   30
He will be back after the war."

The war then was different from the war now.
The war now is *nothing*.

I used to live in London till they burnt it.
What was it like? It was just like here.
No, that's the truth.
My mother would come here, some, but she would cry.
She said to Miss Elise, "He's not himself";
She said, "Don't you love me any more at all?"

I was *myself.*   40
Finally she wouldn't come at all.
She never said one thing my father said, or Sister.
Sometimes she did,
Sometimes she was the same, but that was when I dreamed it.
I could tell I was dreaming, she was just the same.

That Christmas she bought me a toy dog.

I asked her what was its name, and when she didn't know
I asked her over, and when she didn't know
I said, "You're not my mother, you're not my mother.
She *hasn't* gone to Scotland, she is dead!"   50
And she said, "Yes, he's dead, he's dead!"
And cried and cried; she *was* my mother,
She put her arms around me and we cried.

Randall Jarrell

One reads poetry with one's nerves.

Wallace Stevens

The poet...he can make every word he
speaks draw blood.

Walt Whitman

For whatever embryo the poem starts
from—an event, an emotion, a character,
a scene, an insight, an idea—its theme
never exists in isolation.

Elizabeth Drew

Snake

A snake came to my water-trough
On a hot, hot day, and I in pajamas for the heat,
To drink there.

In the deep, strange-scented shade of the great dark carob-tree
I came down the steps with my pitcher
And must wait, must stand and wait, for there he was at the trough
    before me.

He reached down from a fissure in the earth-wall in the gloom
And trailed his yellow-brown slackness soft-bellied down, over
    the edge of the stone trough
And rested his throat upon the stonebottom,
And where the water had dripped from the tap, in a small clearness,   10
He sipped with his straight mouth,
Softly drank through his straight gums, into his slack long body,
Silently.

Someone was before me at my water-trough,
And I, like a second-comer, waiting.

He lifted his head from his drinking, as cattle do,
And looked at me vaguely, as drinking cattle do,
And flickered his two-forked tongue from his lips, and mused a moment,
And stooped and drank a little more,
Being earth-brown, earth-golden from the burning bowels of the earth   20
On the day of Sicilian July, with Etna smoking.

The voice of my education said to me
He must be killed,
For in Sicily the black, black snakes are innocent, the gold are venomous.

And voices in me said, If you were a man
You would take a stick and break him now, and finish him off.

But must I confess how I liked him,
How glad I was he had come like a guest in quiet,to drink at my
    water-trough
And depart peaceful, pacified, and thankless
Into the burning bowels of this earth?   30

Was it cowardice, that I dared not kill him?
Was it perversity, that I longed to talk to him?
Was it humility, to feel honoured?
I felt so honoured.

And yet those voices:
If you were not afraid, you would kill him!

And truly I was afraid, I was most afraid,
But even so, honoured still more
That he should seek my hospitality
From out the dark door of the secret earth.   40

He drank enough
And lifted his head, dreamily, as one who has drunken,
And flickered his tongue like a forked night on the air, so black,
Seeming to lick his lips,
And looked around like a god, unseeing, into the air,
And slowly turned his head,
And slowly, very slowly, as if thrice adream
Proceeded to draw his slow length curving round
And climb again the broken bank of my wall-face.

And as he put his head into that dreadful hole,   50
And as he slowly drew up, snake-easing his shoulders, and entered farther,
A sort of horror, a sort of protest against his withdrawing into that horrid
     black hole,
Deliberately going into the blackness, and slowly drawing himself after,
Overcame me now his back was turned.

I looked round, I put down my pitcher,
I picked up a clumsy log,
And threw it at the water trough with a clatter.

I think it did not hit him,
But suddenly that part of him that was left behind convulsed in undignified
     haste,
Writhed like lightning, and was gone   60
Into the black hole, the earth-lipped fissure in the wall-front,
At which, in the intense still noon, I stared with fascination.

And immediately I regretted it.
I thought how paltry, how vulgar, what a mean act!
I despised myself and the voices of my accursed human education.

And I thought of the albatross,
And I wished he would come back, my snake.

For he seemed to me again like a king,
Like a king in exile, uncrowned in the underworld,
Now due to be crowned again.   70

And so, I missed my chance with one of the lords
Of life.
And I have something to expiate;
A pettiness.

D. H. Lawrence

221

Patterns

I walk down the garden paths,
And all the daffodils
Are blowing, and the bright blue squills.
I walk down the patterned garden paths
In my stiff, brocaded gown.
With my powdered hair and jewelled fan,
I too am a rare
Pattern, as I wander down
The garden paths.

My dress is richly figured,   10
And the train
Makes a pink and silver stain
On the gravel, and the thrift
Of the borders.
Just a plate of current fashion
Tripping by in high-heeled, ribboned shoes.
Not a softness anywhere about me,
Only whalebone and brocade.
And I sink on a seat in the shade
Of a lime tree. For my passion   20
Wars against the stiff brocade.
The daffodils and squills
Flutter in the breeze
As they please.
And I weep;
For the lime tree is in blossom
And one small flower has dropped upon my bosom.

And the plashing of waterdrops
In the marble fountain
Comes down the garden paths.   30
The dripping never stops.
Underneath my stiffened gown
Is the softness of a woman bathing in a marble basin,
A basin in the midst of hedges grown
So thick, she cannot see her lover hiding,
But she guesses he is near,
And the sliding of the water
Seems the stroking of a dear
Hand upon her.
What is Summer in a fine brocaded gown!   40
I should like to see it lying in a heap upon the ground.
All the pink and silver crumpled up on the ground.

I would be the pink and silver as I ran along the paths,
And he would stumble after,
Bewildered by my laughter.
I should see the sun flashing from his sword-hilt and the buckles on
    his shoes.
I would choose
To lead him in a maze along the patterned paths,
A bright and laughing maze for my heavy-booted lover.
Till he caught me in the shade,   50
And the buttons of his waistcoat bruised my body as he clasped me,
Aching, melting, unafraid.
With the shadows of the leaves and the sundrops,
And the plopping of the waterdrops,
All about us in the open afternoon—
I am very like to swoon
With the weight of this brocade,
For the sun sifts through the shade.

Underneath the fallen blossom
In my bosom,   60
Is a letter I have hid.
It was brought to me this morning by a rider from the Duke.
"Madam, we regret to inform you that Lord Hartwell
Died in action Thursday se'nnight."
As I read it in the white, morning sunlight,
The letters squirmed like snakes.
"Any answer, Madam," said my footman.
"No," I told him.
"See that the messenger takes some refreshment
No, no answer."   70
And I walked into the garden,
Up and down the patterned paths,
In my stiff, correct brocade.
The blue and yellow flowers stood up proudly in the sun,
Each one.
I stood upright too,
Held rigid to the pattern
By the stiffness of my gown.
Up and down I walked.
Up and down.   80

In a month he would have been my husband.
In a month, here, underneath this lime,
We would have broken the pattern;
He for me, and I for him,
He as Colonel, I as Lady,
On this shady seat.
He had a whim
That sunlight carried blessing.
And I answered, "It shall be as you have said."
Now he is dead.   90

In Summer and in Winter I shall walk
Up and down
The patterned garden paths
In my stiff, brocaded gown.
The squills and daffodils
Will give place to pillared roses, and to asters and to snow.
I shall go
Up and down,
In my gown.
Gorgeously arrayed,   100
Boned and stayed.
And the softness of my body will be guarded from embrace
By each button, hook, and lace.
For the man who should loose me is dead,
Fighting with the Duke in Flanders,
In a pattern called a war.
Christ! What are patterns for?

Amy Lowell

*I need scarcely observe that a poem deserves its title
inasmuch as it excites, by elevating the soul. The
value of the poem is in the ratio of this elevating
excitement.*

Edgar Allan Poe

A Field of Light

1

Came to lakes; came to dead water,
Ponds with moss and leaves floating,
Planks sunk in the sand.

A log turned at the touch of a foot;
A long weed floated upward;
An eye tilted.

> Small winds made
> A chilly noise;
> The softest cove
> Cried for sound.   10

> Reached for a grape
> And the leaves changed;
> A stone's shape
> Became a clam.

> A fine rain fell
> On fat leaves;
> I was there alone
> In a watery drowse.

2

Angel within me, I asked,
Did I ever curse the sun?   20
Speak and abide.

> Under, under the sheaves,
> Under the blackened leaves,
> Behind the green viscid trellis,
> In the deep grass at the edge of a field,
> Along the low ground dry only in August, —

Was it dust I was kissing?
A sigh came far.
Alone, I kissed the skin of a stone;
Marrow-soft, danced in the sand.   30

3

The dirt left my hand, visitor.
I could feel the mare's nose.
A path went walking.
The sun glittered on a small rapids.
Some morning thing came, beating its wings.
The great elm filled with birds.

Listen, love,
The fat lark sang in the field;
I touched the ground, the ground warmed by
   the killdeer,
The salt laughed and the stones;   40
The ferns had their ways, and the pulsing lizards,
And the new plants, still awkward in their soil,
The lovely diminutives.
I could watch! I could watch!
I saw the separateness of all things!
My heart lifted up with the great grasses;
The weeds believed me, and the nesting birds.
There were clouds making a rout of shapes crossing a
   windbreak of cedars,
And a bee shaking drops from a rain-soaked honeysuckle.
The worms were delighted as wrens.   50
And I walked, I walked through the light air;
I moved with the morning.

Theodore Roethke

*A poet is, before anything else, a person who is
passionately in love with language.*

W. H. Auden

Poetry is not a thing said but a way of saying it.

A. E. Housman

A poem should not mean but be.

Archibald Macleish

Poem in October

It was my thirtieth year to heaven
Woke to my hearing from harbour and neighbour wood
   And the musselpooled and the heron-
      Priested shore
     The morning beckon
With water praying and call of seagull and rook
And the knock of sailing boats on the net-webbed wall
   Myself to set foot
     That second
In the still sleeping town and set forth.   10

My birthday began with the water-
Birds and the birds of the winged trees flying my name
   Above the farms and the white horses
      And I rose
     In rainy autumn
And walked abroad in a shower of all my days.
High tide and the heron dived when I took the road
   Over the border
     And the gates
Of the town closed as the town awoke.   20

A springful of larks in a rolling
Cloud and the roadside bushes brimming with whistling
   Blackbirds and the sun of October
      Summery
     On the hill's shoulder,
Here were fond climates and sweet singers suddenly
Come in the morning where I wandered and listened
   To the rain-wringing
     Wind blow cold
In the woods faraway under me.   30

Pale rain over the dwindling harbour
And over the sea-wet church the size of a snail
   With its horns through mist and the castle
      Brown as owls
     But all the gardens
Of spring and summer were blooming in the tall tales
Beyond the border and under the lark-full cloud.
   There could I marvel
     My birthday
Away but the weather turned around.   40

It turned away from the blithe country,
And down the other air and the blue altered sky
   Streamed again a wonder of summer
      With apples
     Pears and red currants,
And I saw in the turning so clearly a child's
Forgotten mornings when he walked with his mother
   Through the parables
   Of sunlight
And the legends of the green chapels   50

   And the twicetold fields of infancy
That his tears burned my cheeks and his heart moved in mine.
   These were the woods the river and sea
     Where a boy
    In the listening
Summertime of the dead whispered the truth of his joy
To the trees and the stones and the fish in the tide.
   And the mystery
    Sang alive
Still in the water and singing birds.   60

   And there could I marvel my birthday
Away but the weather turned around. And the true
   Joy of the long-dead child sang burning
    In the sun.
   It was my thirtieth
Year to heaven stood there then in the summer noon
Though the town below lay leaved with October blood.
   O may my heart's truth
    Still be sung
On this high hill in a year's turning.   70

Dylan Thomas

Aesthetics
The study of the beautiful.

Alphabet Poem
A poem using the linear order of the letters of the alphabet at the start of each line. Usually the poet works with only a portion of the alphabet:
Age
Birth
Coffin
Desire
Eternity

Allegory
The characters and events of a narrative suggest and correspond to the details of an archetypal story, such as a Greek myth or a biblical story. The secondary, or higher, meaning runs parallel to the surface story. See "The Carpenter's Son" by A. E. Housman.

Alliteration
The repetition of initial sounds in words.
"Whip at typhoon speed past ticket takers"
Joy Kogawa

Allusion
A reference to something or some person from literature, religious lore, or history. T. S. Eliot's poem "The Hollow Men" begins with two allusions. The first, "Mistah Kurtz — he dead," refers to the novel *Heart of Darkness* by Joseph Conrad.

Anapest
(⌣⌣╱) (interrupt) Two short syllables followed by a stressed syllable. The metre of the limerick.

Antithesis
Contrasting ideas expressed in a balanced grammatical structure.
"The best lack all conviction, while the worst/Are full of passionate intensity."
William Butler Yeats

Apostrophe
To address a person or thing not present as if it were present.
"O world, I shall be buried all over Ontario."
Michael Ondaatje

Archetype
("the original type") A basic pattern or concept common to people of different times and cultures. For example, most peoples have a traditional creation story.

Art Trouvé
Found art. Found poetry. Ready-made art. Anti-art. Poems made from newspaper headlines and other non-poetic print are a form of art trouvé.

Artistic Click
What the reader experiences when the elements of the poem snap into place and make perfect sense. The feeling of understanding that engenders inspiration.

Assonance
Repetition of the same vowel sound in a line of poetry.
"In zones of silence they grow tall and slow,"
P. K. Page

Atmosphere
See mood.

Audience
Those who watch, read, listen, enjoy, judge. The people for whom the work was intended.

Audio
(Latin = I hear) Audio refers to the sound portion of a film, a TV broadcast — or a poem. How does the poem speak?

Avant-garde
(French = advance guard) The term refers to those artists who are innovators in thought, style, and form. See the poems by e. e. cummings, which are considered avant-garde even today, decades after they were written.

Ballad
A narrative poem, originally composed to be sung. There are folk ballads and literary ballads. See pages 106-109.

Black Humour
In literature, a style of writing that derives humour from serious topics such as cruelty, insanity, murder, death, and other painful realities. See "Earth" by John Hall Wheelock.

Blank Verse
Unrhymed iambic pentametre. This verse form is closest to the natural cadences of English speech. Shakespeare used blank verse in his plays.

Blues
An American style of musical expression originating among the blacks of the deep south in the U.S.A. Blues songs deal with such elemental themes as love, betrayal, work, and celebration. Key phrases are repeated throughout the song. Many rock songs draw upon the blues tradition.

Cacophony
The use of sounds that are unpleasant to the ear. "Glut," "hiss," and "spit" are examples. See Wifred Owen's "Dulce Et Decorum Est."

Canto
The main divisions of a long poem. A canto is to poetry what a chapter is to a prose work.

Chorus
A line or stanza that is regularly repeated throughout a song. A chorus is the musical equivalent of a refrain.

Computer Poetry
The poet takes a word or phrase and works toward a readout. Each line of the poem consists of letters selected from the initial word or phrase; each letter remains in its original position. See pages 132-135.

Concrete Poetry
Poetry that places attention on the concrete material out of which the poem is made — letters and words. The appeal is to the visual, phonetic, and kinetic. See pages 128-131.

Connotation
The aura, the field of association, surrounding the word. For example, in the ballad "The Twa Corbies," the word "hound" specifies a kind of dog, but it also suggests, or connotes, the qualities of devotion and loyalty.

Consonance
The repetition of identical consonant sounds. "Then down a green plain leaping, laughing, they run," William Blake

Convention
A time-honoured way of doing something. By convention, a limerick has five lines.

Corporate Computer Poetry
A form of computer poetry. An editor takes readouts created by two or more writers from the same starting point, and arranges the readouts in an interesting order. See pages 134-135.

Couplet
Two lines of poetry that rhyme.

cummingese
A word coined to describe the poetic language developed by Edward Estlin Cummings (1894-1962). Cummings wrote poems for the eye as well as the ear. See pages 124-127.

Curtal Sonnet
A sonnet form devised by Gerard Manley Hopkins in 1877. A curtal sonnet has 11 lines — one section of 6 lines and another section of 4 1/2 lines. It is a shortened, or curtailed, form of the traditional 14-line sonnet. See "Pied Beauty" by Hopkins.

Dactyl
($\diagup \cup \cup$) (merrily) A dactyllic foot contains three syllables, with the accent on the first syllable.

Denotation
The exact dictionary definition of a word.

Dialect
The language of a special group or class of people. "To a Mouse" by Robert Burns is written in the Scottish dialect of 1785.

Dialogue
A conversation, a talking to each other. A. E. Housman's "'Is My Team Ploughing'" is written as a dialogue between a dead man and his living friend.

Diction
The words the poet chooses to express his or her meaning. A good poet selects each word carefully, for a particular reason.

Didactic Verse
Verse written to instruct or teach. See Patrick Lane's "The Bird."

Disc Poetry
Songs that have poetic merit that one hears on the radio airwaves or on CDs, cassettes, and records. See pages 185-199.

Doggerel
Light, crude, carelessly written verse.

Dramatic Monologue
The dramatic monologue has a character (not the poet) speaking to one or more people. Reading a dramatic monologue is like hearing only one side of a conversation. See Robert Browning's "My Last Duchess."

Dysphemism
A crude or shocking word or expression used in place of socially accepted language. The opposite of euphemism.

Elegy
A lyric poem of a mournful nature written about someone's death. "She Dwelt among the Untrodden Ways," by William Wordsworth, is elegiac.

Emotive Language
Language that evokes an emotional response in the reader. The language of poetry is emotive. Poetry makes reference to facts and depicts objects and situations, but it also strongly appeals to attitudes and feelings.

End-Stopped Verse
The flow of the poem is stopped at the end of each line by a punctuation mark, or by the phrasing of the sentence.
"Morning has broken like the first morning,
Blackbird has spoken like the first word."
Eleanor Farjeon

English Sonnet
See Shakespearean sonnet.

Enjambement
The syntax or the cadence of a line of poetry carries the reader into the next line. An alternative to end-stopped verse.
"Then grinning, he reached with his freckled wrist/And drew me up after." Earle Birney

Epic
A long narrative poem. The *Illiad* and the *Odyssey* by Homer are well-known epics.

Epigram
A very short poem, often consisting of two rhyming lines. Epigrams are usually satirical, wise, or witty. See page 121.

Epiphany
A moment of sudden insight or revelation. See Alden Nowlan's "Johnnie's Poem."

Epitaph
An inscription on a tombstone. A poem about the dead. A short poem written to be inscribed on a tombstone.

Euphemism
The use of a pleasant-sounding word or phrase to avoid talking about the unpleasant reality.
"Die" is the precise real word. Euphemisms for die are "passed away," "gone to his reward," "no longer with us."

Euphony
The use of sounds pleasing to the ear. The combination of pleasant sounds in speech, poetry, or music.
"The woods are lovely, dark and deep."
Robert Frost

Eye Rhyme
Words that rhyme to the eye but not to the ear: stood/blood; gave/have; loves/moves.

Facsimile
An exact copy or reproduction of a manuscript. There is a facsimile of Robert Frost's "Stopping by Woods" on page 71.

Feminine Rhyme
Rhymes of two syllables are called feminine rhymes: deliver/quiver; grieving/believing.

Figurative Language
Heightened, imaginative language, characterized by simile, metaphor, personification, and so on.
"Thunda from a bass drum sounding/lightning from a trumpet and a organ,"
Linton Kwesi Johnson

Flashback
A pause in the narrative flow to relate events from the past. These retreats to the past have a bearing on the present situation. See Randall Jarrell's poem "The Truth."

Foil
Contrast in character, setting, or action. The writer emphasizes or enhances one character's traits by playing him or her off against a character with opposite qualities. See "Mr. Flood's Party," by Edwin Arlington Robinson.

Foot
The smallest combination of accented and unaccented syllables in a line of poetry. A line of verse usually has several feet. Tetrametre – 4 feet. Pentametre = 5 feet. See Rhythm, p. 77.

Foreshadowing
Indicating or suggesting before it happens what will occur later in the work of art.

Form
The pattern or the structure of the poem; the way the poem is put together. Some poems take the form of a story, a narrative. Others are structured like a dialogue or an argument. Others like a work of music. Others are put together in a more intuitive way, in a succession of related images, for example. Form ≠ genre.

Frame Story
A story that is outside the main story. See "The Witch of Coös," by Robert Frost.

Free Verse
(also known as vers libre) Free verse follows the natural cadences of the language and discards traditional metre, rhyme, and stanza patterns. See D. H. Lawrence's "Snake."

Genre
A certain kind of literature or poetry. The novel is a literary genre. Poetic genres include the sonnet, the epigram, the lyric, and the haiku. (See Poetic Genres, pages 104–135.) Each genre is characterized by a set of rules or conventions that provides the parameters of the poem. Genre is a convenient but sometimes misleading and unhelpful way of classifying poetry. Is Frank Sidgwick's poem "Aeronaut to His Lady" a sonnet?

Gothic
The atmosphere of the horror story, replete with ghosts, mystery, horrible happenings, and the macabre. "The Garden of the Thieves" by Gwendolyn MacEwen has a hint of the gothic.

Haiku
Originally a form of Japanese poetry. The haiku is usually written in 3 lines, containing 17 syllables. The organization of syllables (5-7-5) represents one flowing out of the spirit into one exhalation of breath. See pages 118-119.

Hyperbole
Obvious exaggeration of the facts either for a comic or serious effect. See Robert Burns's poem "O My Luve's Like a Red, Red Rose."

Iamb
(◡ ⁄)(destroy) An iambic foot has two syllables, with the stress on the second syllable. Iambic rhythm is the most common metre in English poetry.

Image
A word-picture. An appeal to the reader's senses and imagination.

Imagery
All the images in the poem considered as a whole. A poem's imagery creates a certain mood. It suggests to the reader what to think and feel, often very subtly.

Imagism
The use of clear, exact, colourful images that appeal to the senses. You can see, touch, hear, and feel an imagist poem. See the poems of Amy Lowell.

"in medias res"
Many works of art tell a story, but sometimes the artist doesn't want to begin at the beginning or end at the end. "In medias res" is a Latin expression meaning "in the middle of things," which is where some narratives start.

Inscape
A term created by Gerard Manley Hopkins (1844-1889) to express the "thisness" of something. Everything in creation has its own distinctive character, which makes it unique. This is inscape.

Instress
A term from the journals of Gerard Manley Hopkins. He invented the term to describe the inner pressure or urge that directs a thing to pursue its proper function. Instress is inherent in all things. See Hopkins's poem "God's Grandeur."

Interior Monologue
One person's inner thoughts and feelings. The flow of thoughts or the stream of consciousness is sometimes linear and sometimes a non-linear weaving of inner realities. See Amy Lowell's poem "Patterns."

Irony
Irony occurs when someone says something but the reverse is true, or when a situation appears to be one way but instead is exactly the opposite. In this excerpt from "Ex-basketball Player" by John Updike, the ironic twist comes in the last line: "Flick seldom speaks to Mae, just sits and nods Beyond her face towards bright applauding tiers Of Necco Wafers, Nibs, and Juju Beads."

Italian Sonnet
See Petrarchan sonnet.

Juxtaposition
The poet puts two or more things side-by-side, even though they usually aren't associated with one another. The poet creates the juxtaposition without explaining it. The reader has to employ his or her imagination to guess at the poet's motives. Note the second line in this quotation from Andrei Voznesenky's "Phone Booth": "What do you want? A bushel of rhymes or so? An autograph? A bone?"

Lampoon
A poem that satirizes a person by sketching a malicious character portrait. See Raymond Souster's "Willie the Lion."

Light Verse
Poetry whose main purpose is to delight and entertain. Popular light verse forms are the epigram and the limerick. See pages 96-101.

Limerick
A five-line poem rhyming aabba and written in anapestic metre. This verse form has been popular since the 1846 publication of Edward Lear's Book of Nonsense Verse. See page 120.

Literal
An interpretation of a poem not going beyond the actual facts. An interpretation based wholly on the actual meaning of the words and lines. A literal interpretation ignores the potential of figurative language, imagery, symbolism, and leaps of imagination.

Lyric
A broad poetic category or genre. A lyric is a short poem expressing a personal feeling, emotion, or attitude about some topic. Many poems can therefore be classified as lyric — sonnets, elegies, free-verse poems, and so on.

Masculine Rhyme
Single-syllable rhymes are masculine rhymes: light/night; song/wrong.

Metaphor
A comparison between two unlike things. The poet actually identifies one thing with another, asserting that they are the same.
"A poem is a small machine made out of words." William Carlos Williams

Metre
Metre (measure) depends on the number of feet in a given line of poetry. Rhythm is determined by the pattern of stressed and unstressed syllables in a line of poetry. See Rhythm, page 77.

Metonymy
(Greek = a change of name) A kind of metaphor. An object is given the name of something else with which it is associated. John Milton, referring to his fading eyesight, writes "When I consider how my light is spent."

Mime
To act out a scene or situation without using any words. The story is related to the audience by means of facial expression, gesture, and body movement.

Minimalism
"Less is more." The poem is reduced to its basic, most direct expression. No unnecessary words or images clutter the picture. See the poems of William Carlos Williams.

Monologue
The poet creates a character; the poem is the character's "speech" to the reader. See page 93. See also Interior monologue.

Mood
Mood is the emotional environment, or atmosphere, created by the poet. A good poet, like Anne Sexton, can create a mood with a very few words: "A thousand doors ago/when I was a lonely kid…"

Motif
In literature, architecture, music, home decoration a basic recurring theme, pattern, or idea. Motifs help to unify the diverse elements of a work of art.

Muses
In literature, "muses" or "muse" refers to poetic inspiration. The Muses were Greek goddesses who presided over poetry, music, dance, and the arts.

Narrative
The story-line of the poem. A narrative poem is a poem written to tell a particular story. Many poems have very little or no narrative.

Neologism
A new word or phrase. Using old words in new ways. The neologism "Goldengrove unleaving," invented by Gerard Manley Hopkins in his poem "To Margaret," is a poetic way of describing trees losing their leaves in autumn.

Nick
Many poems have a "nick," a particular word, phrase, line, or stanza that grabs the reader's eye and imagination, and charges the rest of the poem with meaning.

Nom de Plume
(French = pen name) (pseudonym) A fictitious name assumed by an author. T. S. Eliot sometimes used the nom de plume "Old Possum."

Nonsense Verse
Light-hearted verse that delights as it entertains. Often the topics are silly and the rhymes ridiculous. See Ogden Nash's poems.

Objective Correlative
A concrete object is used to suggest a certain emotion.
"I have measured out my life in coffee spoons." T. S. Eliot.

Octave
The first part (8 lines) of a Petrarchan sonnet.

Ode
A lyric on a serious subject characterized by dignity of style.

Onomatopoeia
The sound of the word mimics the sound to which it refers: "thud," "crackle," "buzz," and "chickadee" are onomatopoeic.

Oxymoron
(Greek: oxy = sharp, moros = dull) An expression that combines contradictory or opposite ideas.

Paradox
An apparently contradictory statement, with an element of truth in it.

Parody
A comic imitation of a serious poem. See pages 102-103.

Pastoral
A poem glorifying and idealizing rural life and nature. See "Ode on Solitude" by Alexander Pope.

Pathetic Fallacy
An artistic device. Nature reflects the feelings of the characters and the mood of the events in the story. See Andrei Voznesensky's "First Ice."

Persona
One of the most important literary concepts. The persona who narrates, or speaks, the poem is not the living person who wrote the poem. In writing the poem, the poet always creates a persona, a speaker who is other than himself or herself. Sometimes the two resemble one another and the reader can make a connection between them. More often, the poet is assuming a role to express a special point of view.

Personification
To attribute to inanimate objects, animals, or abstract ideas the characteristics and qualities of persons.
"Or I guess the grass is itself a child, the produced babe of the vegetation." Walt Whitman

Petrarchan Sonnet
Also called the Italian sonnet. It consists of 14 lines divided into an octave (8 lines) rhyming abba abba and a sestet (6 lines) rhyming cde cde or cdcdcd. In the octave the poet sketches the scene and in the sestet he or she makes a comment or observation. See John Milton's "On His Blindness."

Poetic Justice
Justice as one wishes it to be. The good are rewarded and the evil are punished.

Poetics
The portion of literary criticism concerned with poetry. The title of Aristotle's study of poetic drama.

Point of View
The way in which something is presented, viewed, or considered. The poet's mental attitude. The tone the poet adopts in presenting the material.

Pun
A play on words; words identical or similar in sound but different in meaning. There is a pun in the last line of Stacy Kozakavich's poem "The Knitting Club":
"I let her string her own yarns."

Quatrain
A stanza of four lines. Quatrains are the most familiar of English verse forms. See page 105.

Reader
"I write half the poem. The reader writes the other half." Paul Valéry

Realism
The artist chooses to present life as it actually is, without exaggeration or disguise.

Refrain
Lines of poetry that are repeated at regular intervals within the poem. A refrain sometimes consists of a single line or even a single word. See also chorus.

Rhyme
A combining agent that glues the lines of the poem together by similarity of sounds. Rhyme depends on sound not on spelling: crime/rhyme/slime/time. See page 76.

Rhythm
The flow of the words and the lines of the poem. The recurrent beat or stress of the line. When the rhythm of a poem is regular, it is called metre. See page 77.

Satire
A work of literature exposing the follies and weaknesses of a person or institution. Satire endeavours to bring about reform by ridiculing human frailities and customs. See Tom Wayman's "Picketing Supermarkets."

Sestet
The second part (6 lines) of a Petrarchan sonnet.

Shakespearean Sonnet
Also called the English sonnet. A poem consisting of 14 lines with three quatrains (rhyming abab cdcd efef) followed by a rhyming couplet (gg). See Shakespeare's "Sonnet 29."

Simile
A comparison between two things of unlike nature usually introduced by like, as, or than. "hands as smooth as marble and naked as the morning," Mary Di Michele

Shape Poetry
Also called pattern poetry. The lines of the poem are arranged in the shape of the subject of the poem. See George Herbert's "The Altar."

Slice-of-life
An anecdotal sketch of life just as it is without adornment or enlargement.

Song
A poem written to be sung.

Sonnet
A poem of fourteen lines. There are many different variations of the sonnet form, but the two usual types are the Petrarchan (Italian) and the Shakespearean (English). See pages 110-113.

Sonnet Sequence
A series of sonnets written by one poet on a particular theme or topic. Sonnet sequences have been written by Sir Philip Sidney, William Shakespeare, and Elizabeth Barrett Browning.

Spondee
($\prime\prime$) (heartbreak) A metrical foot consisting of two accented syllables together.

Stanza
The pattern of lines that makes up a unit of the poem. The most common stanza is the quatrain (units of four lines).

Stream of consciousness
See Interior monologue.

Structure
The way the poem is put together. See form.

Surrealism
("above realism") An artistic movement that originated in France in the 1920s. The Surrealists said that true art and creativity come from the subconscious. Surrealist art and writing are irrational and dreamlike. Narrative is abandoned in favour of ungoverned imagery. See Sylvia Plath's "Mirror" for a poem with an element of the surreal.

Symbol
Something that suggests or stands for something else. There are natural symbols, conventional symbols, and private symbols. See page 84.

Symbolism
Poems are suggestive. They reach beyond themselves. For example, when a poem refers to the spring season, the reader is reminded of many associated experiences and images: the renewal of vegetation, the happiness that seems to come with the season, the cycle of life, the idea of an afterlife. Each poem has its own symbolism. Compare "Spring" by Gerard Manley Hopkins with "Spring" by Edna St. Vincent Millay.

Synecdoche
A part of something signifies the whole.

Tercet
A three-line stanza.

Theme
The meaning, the point, the gist, the essence of a piece of literature.

Title
Never take a poem's title for granted. A poet often uses the title to add an extra layer of meaning or an ironic reversal. See "I, Icarus" by Alden Nowlan.

Tone
The artist's attitude towards the subject of his or her poem and towards the audience. Tone ≠ mood. A poem might have a gothic mood but a satiric tone. Tone can be difficult to assess; the reader must gauge the storyteller's voice and intent.

Triple Rhyme
Three syllables similar in sound: million/vermilion.

Trochee
($\prime\smile$) (spirit) A trochaic foot consists of two syllables with the accent or stress on the first syllable.

Verse
A single line of poetry is also known as a verse. The word "verse" is sometimes used to signify poetry that does not have a serious intent — e.g., light verse.

Video
(Latin = I see) Video refers to the picture portion of a film or television broadcast — or a poem. How does the poem make a picture?

Villanelle
A most rigid form employing 19 lines with only 2 rhymes throughout the poem. A villanelle consists of 5 sets of 3 lines (tercets) and a concluding quatrain. Lines 1, 6, 12, and 18 are the same. Lines 3, 9, 15 and 19 are the same. See Dylan Thomas's "Do Not Go Gentle into That Good Night."

Zeitgeist
(German = time spirit) The spirit, the preoccupation, of a special period or era. See William Butler Yeats's poem "The Second Coming."

This index does not include poems with anonymous authors, nor does it include poems that were written by students and published here for the first time. For poems by students, see Student Voices, page 241. For a complete index, see Index of Titles, page 242.

BIOGRAMS

BIOGRAMS

in order of appearance

INDEX OF TITLES

ACKNOWLEDGEMENTS

MILTON ACORN "Islanders" "July Creatures" "The Miner's Wife" reprinted by permission of the author's literary executor.

"THE ALGEBRA OF THE HEART" reprinted by permission of the authors.

LAURIE ANDERSON "O Superman (for Massenet)" by Laurie Anderson © 1982, Difficult Music (BMI).

MARGARET ATWOOD "This Is a Photograph of Me" "The Islands" from The Circle Game, copyright © 1966 Margaret Atwood (Toronto: House of Anansi Press). Reprinted by permission. "Dream 2: Brian the Still-Hunter" from The Journals of Susanna Moodie, © Oxford University Press Canada 1970. "It Is Dangerous to Read Newspapers" "Progressive Insanities of a Pioneer" from Selected Poems, selection © Margaret Atwood 1976. Reprinted by permission of Oxford University Press Canada.

W.H. AUDEN "Ballad" from Collected Poems reprinted by permission of Faber and Faber Ltd.

MARGARET AVISON "Tennis" from Winter Sun by Margaret Avison. Used by permission of the Canadian Publishers, McClelland and Stewart, Toronto.

E.J. BARRY "The Hitch-hiker" "Lunch Counter" "MADMEN" "SMOKING" reprinted by permission of the author.

HILAIRE BELLOC "Fatigue" reprinted by permission of the Peters Fraser & Dunlop Group Ltd.

STEPHEN VINCENT BENET "The Knockout" from Heaven and Earth by Stephen Vincent Benét. Copyright 1924 by Stephen Vincent Benét. Copyright renewed © 1951 by Rosemary Carr Benét. Reprinted by permission of Brandt & Brandt Literary Agents, Inc.

JOHN BETJEMAN "A Subaltern's Love-Song" from Collected Poems, reprinted by permission of John Murray (Publishers) Ltd.

AMBROSE BIERCE "Epigram" (definition) from The Enlarged Devil's Dictionary. Reprinted by permission of Doubleday, a division of Bantam, Doubleday, Dell Publishing Group, Inc.

EARLE BIRNEY "Canada: Case History" "David" from The Collected Poems of Earle Birney. Used by permission of the Canadian Publishers, McClelland and Stewart, Toronto.

ROO BORSON "Grey Glove" reprinted by permission of the author. "The Wind, Growing Up" from The Whole Night, Coming Home by Roo Borson. Used by permission of the Canadian Publishers, McClelland and Stewart, Toronto.

GEORGE BOWERING "The Blue" used by permission of the Canadian Publishers, McClelland and Stewart, Toronto.

ELIZABETH BREWSTER "Poem for an Audience of One" reprinted by permission of the author.

GWENDOLYN BROOKS "We Real Cool" "Sadie and Maud" from Blacks © 1987. Published by The David Company: Chicago. Reprinted by permission of the author. "First Fight. Then Fiddle." reprinted by permission of the author.

ALDO BRUNO "Immigrant" reprinted by permission of the author.

BUSON "The Sudden Chillness" by Buson from An Introduction to Haiku by Harold G. Henderson. Copyright © 1958 by Harold G. Henderson. Reprinted by permission of Doubleday, a division of Bantam, Doubleday, Dell Publishing Group, Inc.

G.K. CHESTERTON "The Donkey" from Collected Poems published by J.M. Dent.

BRUCE COCKBURN "Wondering Where the Lions Are" © 1979 Golden Mountain Music Corp. Words and music by Bruce Cockburn. Taken from the album Dancing in the Dragon's Jaws. "World of Wonders" © 1985 Golden Mountain Music Corp. Words and music by Bruce Cockburn. Taken from the album World of Wonders.

LEONARD COHEN "For Anne" "Another Night with Telescope" from Selected Poems by Leonard Cohen. Used by permission of the Canadian Publishers, McClelland and Stewart, Toronto.

JOHN ROBERT COLOMBO "Absurd Limerick" reprinted from Colombo's Little Book of Canadian Proverbs (Edmonton: Hurtig Publishers, 1979), edited by John Robert Colombo. Reprinted by permission of the editor.

E.E. CUMMINGS "anyone lived in a pretty how town" reprinted by permission of Liveright Publishing Company. "55" "maybe god" "12" "one" reprinted from Xiape by E.E. Cummings, edited by George James Firmage, by permission of Liveright Publishing Corporation. Copyright 1950 by E.E. Cummings. Copyright © 1979, 1978, 1973 by Nancy T. Andrews. Copyright © 1979, 1973 by George James Firmage.

AUGUSTO DE CAMPOS "sem um numero" reprinted by permission of Indiana University Press.

MARY DI MICHELE "As in the Beginning" is reprinted from Necessary Sugar by permission of Oberon Press.

EMILY DICKINSON "The Sky is low" "I like to see it lap the Miles" "Apparently with no surprise" "After great pain" " 'Faith' is a fine invention" "Because I could not stop for Death" "Hope is a subtle glutton" "This is my letter to the world" reprinted by permission of the publishers and the Trustees of Amherst College from The Poems of Emily Dickinson, edited by Thomas H. Johnson, Cambridge, Mass.: The Belknap Press of Harvard University Press, Copyright 1951, © 1955, 1979, 1983 by The President and Fellows of Harvard College.

GREG DOSMAN "INDIVIDUALIZATION" reprinted by permission of the author.

LOUIS DUDEK "Tree in a Street" "Poetry for Intellectuals" reprinted by permission of the author.

T.S. ELIOT "The Hollow Men" "The Love Song of J. Alfred Prufrock" from Collected Poems 1904-1962 reprinted by permission of Faber & Faber Limited.

MARI EVANS "Where Have You Gone" from I Am a Black Woman, published by Wm. Morrow & Co., 1970. Reprinted by permission of the author.

GEORGE FALUDY "East and West" reprinted by permission of the author.

ELEANOR FARJEON "Morning Has Broken" reprinted by permission of Harold Ober Associates Incorporated. Copyright © 1957 by Eleanor Farjeon.

ROBERT FROST " 'Out, Out—' " "Stopping by Woods on a Snowy Evening" copyright 1916, 1923 by Holt, Rinehart and Winston, Inc. and renewed 1944, 1951 by Robert Frost. "The Draft Horse" copyright © 1962 by Robert Frost. "In Divés Dive" copyright 1936 by Robert Frost and renewed 1964 by Lesley Frost Ballantine. "The Witch of Coös" Copyright 1923 by Holt, Rinehart and Winston and renewed 1951 by Robert Frost. Reprinted from The Poetry of Robert Frost, edited by Edward Connery Lathem, by permission of Henry Holt and Company, Inc.

"The Mother's Song" is reprinted from Poems of the Inuit , edited by John Robert Colombo by permission of Oberon Press.

OGDEN NASH "The Turtle" "Lather as You Go" from Verses from 1929 On by Ogden Nash. "Lather as You Go" copyright 1942 by Ogden Nash. "The Turtle" copyright 1940 by Ogden Nash. "Song of the Open Road" copyright 1932 by Ogden Nash. First appeared in The New Yorker. By permission of Little, Brown and Company.

bp NICHOL "Blues" from LOVE: A Book of Remembrances © 1974 bp Nichol; Talon Books Ltd., Vancouver, Canada.

JEANNETTE NICHOLS "Fast Run in the Junkyard" from Mostly People by Jeannette Nichols. Copyright © 1966 by Rutgers University. Reprinted with permission of Rutgers University Press.

ALDEN NOWLAN "The Masks of Love" "I, Icarus" from Bread, Wine and Salt by Alden Nowlan. "Johnnie's Poem" from Between Tears and Laughter by Alden Nowlan. Reprinted with the permission of Irwin Publishing, Toronto, Ontario. "Two Strangers" "The Execution" "The Bull Moose" reprinted by permission of the author's Estate.

THOMAS O'DONNELL "LISTENING TO PICTURES" reprinted by permission of the author.

PAUL O'NEIL "WATCH YOUR TELEVISION" reprinted by permission of the author.

MICHAEL ONDAATJE "Signature" "Fabulous Shadow" reprinted by permission of the author. "A House Divided" from There's a Trick with a Knife I'm Learning to Do by Michael Ondaatje. Used by permission of the Canadian Publishers, McClelland and Stewart, Toronto.

WILFRED OWEN "Dulce Et Decorum Est" from Collected Poems, edited by C. Day Lewis. Reprinted with permission of the Estate of Wilfred Owen and The Hogarth Press.

P.K. PAGE "T-Bar" © P.K. Page. Used by permission of the author.

DOROTHY PARKER "Song of Perfect Propriety" "One Perfect Rose" "Résumé" from The Portable Dorothy Parker by Dorothy Parker. Copyright 1929, renewed © 1957 by Dorothy Parker. All rights reserved. Reprinted by permission of Viking Penguin Inc.

CHRIS PERRY "APARTHEID" reprinted by permission of the author.

PATRICK PIDDUCK "Titanic Versus Iceberg" reprinted by permission of the author.

AL PITTMAN "Sea Gull" "Faith Healer" "To a Retarded Child Dancing All Alone in an Asphalt School Yard" from Baffles of Wind and Tide by Al Pittman and Clyde Rose. Reprinted by permission of Breakwater Books Ltd.

SYLVIA PLATH "Mirror" from The Collected Poems of Sylvia Plath published by Faber & Faber London. Copyright © 1971, 1981 by Ted Hughes. Reprinted by permission of Olwyn Hughes.

"PORSCHE OR BICYCLE" reprinted by permission of the authors.

EZRA POUND "Meditatio" from Collected Shorter Poems by Ezra Pound. Reprinted by permission of Faber and Faber Ltd. "In a Station of the Metro" from Personae by Ezra Pound. Copyright 1926 by Ezra Pound. Reprinted by permission of New Directions Publishing Corporation.

E.J. PRATT "Sea-Gulls" "The Dying Eagle" from The Collected Poems of E.J. Pratt. Reprinted by permission of University of Toronto Press.

AL PURDY "Joe Barr" from The Collected Poems of Al Purdy. Used by permission of the Canadian Publishers, McClelland and Stewart, Toronto.

HERBERT READ "Night" from Collected Poems published by Faber and Faber Ltd. Reprinted by permission of David Higham Associates Limited.

JAMES REANEY "Winnipeg Seen as a Body of Time and Space" from *Poems*, copyright Canada by James Reaney, 1972 and published by Press Porcépic.

IAN RISWICK "The Scot in a kilt" reprinted by permission of the author.

EDWIN ARLINGTON ROBINSON "Mr. Flood's Party" from Collected Poems by Edwin Arlington Robinson. Copyright 1921 by Edwin Arlington Robinson, renewed 1949 by Ruth Nivison.

THEODORE ROETHKE "My Papa's Waltz" copyright 1942 Hearst Magazines Inc. from The Collected Poems of Theodore Roethke. "A Field of Light" copyright 1948 by The Tiger's Eye. Reprinted by permission of Doubleday, a division of Bantam, Doubleday, Dell Publishing Group, Inc.

JOE ROSENBLATT "Sun Poem" from Top Soil by Joe Rosenblatt. Reprinted by permission of Porcepic Books.

CHRISTINA ROSSETTI "When I am dead, my dearest" from Poetical Works of Christina G. Rossetti (New York: Macmillan, 1924).

CARL SANDBURG "Primer Lesson" from Slabs of the Sunburnt West by Carl Sandburg, copyright 1922 by Harcourt Brace Jovanovich, Inc., renewed 1950 by Carl Sandburg, reprinted by permission of the publisher. "Fog" from Chicago Poems by Carl Sandburg, copyright 1916 by Holt, Rinehart and Winston, Inc., renewed 1944 by Carl Sandburg, reprinted by permission of Harcourt Brace Jovanovich, Inc.

SIEGFRIED SASSOON "Base Details" reprinted by permission of George Sassoon.

F.R. SCOTT "Laurentian Shield" "The Clearing" from Collected Poems by F.R. Scott. Used by permission of the Canadian Publishers, McClelland and Stewart, Toronto.

YAMAGUCHI SEICHI "With a crunching sound" from Modern Japanese Haiku, edited by Makoto Ueda. Reprinted by permission of University of Toronto Press.

ANNE SEXTON "Young" from All My Pretty Ones by Anne Sexton. Copyright © 1962 by Anne Sexton. Reprinted by permission of Houghton Mifflin Company.

KARL SHAPIRO "Auto Wreck" copyright 1942 and renewed 1970 by Karl Shapiro. Reprinted from *Collected Poems 1940-1978* by Karl Shapiro. Reprinted by permission of Random House Inc.

PAUL SIMON "The Boy in the Bubble" © 1986 Paul Simon. "I Am a Rock" copyright © 1965 Paul Simon.

A.J.M. SMITH "To Hold in a Poem" from The Classic Shade: Selected Poems by A.J.M. Smith. Used by permission of the Canadian Publishers, McClelland and Stewart, Toronto.

RAYMOND SOUSTER "Flight of the Roller Coaster" "Death by Streetcar" "A Page from Our History" "The Six-Quart Basket" "I Wanted to Smash" "Church Bells, Montreal" are reprinted from Collected Poems of Raymond Souster by permission of Oberon Press.

"SPLINTERING THE ATOM" reprinted by permission of the authors.

BRUCE SPRINGSTEEN "Wreck on the Highway" © 1980 Bruce Springsteen. Used by permission.

TIFFANY STONE "Hymn" reprinted by permission of the author.

SARA TEASDALE "Thoughts" "The Look" from Collected Poems by Sara Teasdale. Copyright 1915 by Macmillan Publishing Company, renewed 1943 by Mamie T. Wheless.

"TELECONFERENCING" reprinted by permission of the authors.

DYLAN THOMAS "Fern Hill" "Do Not Go Gentle into That Good Night"

"Poem in October" from Collected Poems, published by J.M. Dent. Reprinted by permission of David Higham Associates Limited.

KANEKO TOTA "After a heated argument" from Modern Japanese Haiku, edited by Makota Ueda. Reprinted by permission of University of Toronto Press.

DAVE TURNER "Parody: after Shakespeare" "Shadows" reprinted by permission of the author.

SYLVIA TYSON "Régine" reprinted by permission of the author.

JOHN UPDIKE "Ex-basketball Player" copyright © 1957, 1982 by John Updike. "Mirror" copyright © 1957 by John Updike. "Pendulum" copyright © 1958 by John Updike. From The Carpentered Hen and Other Tame Creatures by John Updike. "Bendix" copyright © 1958 by John Updike. From Telephone Poles and Other Poems by John Updike. Reprinted by permission of Alfred A. Knopf Inc.

UVAVNUK "The Great Sea" is reprinted from Poems of the Inuit edited by John Robert Colombo by permission of Oberon Press.

JEAN VANIER "two prisons divided by a gulf" reprinted by permission of Griffin House Publishers.

SUZANNE VEGA "Small Blue Thing" from the album Suzanne Vega. Reprinted by permission of Waifersong Limited.

ANDREI VOZNESENSKY "First Ice" "Seagull" from Antiworlds and the Fifth Ace, translated by W.H. Auden et al., edited by Patricia Blake and Max Hayward. Reprinted by permission of Schocken Books, published by Pantheon Books, a Division of Random House, Inc. "Phone Booth" from An Arrow in the Wall: Selected Poetry and Prose by Andrei Voznesensky, edited by William Jay Smith and F.D. Reeve. Copyright © 1987 by Henry Holt and Company, Inc. Copyright © 1985, 1986 by Andrei Voznesensky. Reprinted by permission of the publisher.

MIRIAM WADDINGTON "Transformations" "Advice to the Young" from Collected Poems, © Miriam Waddington 1986; reprinted by permission of Oxford University Press Canada.

TOM WAYMAN "Highway 16/5 Illumination" "Picketing Supermarkets" reprinted by permission of the author.

PHYLLIS WEBB "And in Our Time" "Sitting" and the excerpt from "Non Linear" are reprinted by permission of the author.

JOHN HALL WHEELOCK "Earth" reprinted by permission of Charles Scribner's Sons, an imprint of Macmillan Publishing Company, from The Gardener and Other Poems by John Hall Wheelock. © John Hall Wheelock 1961.

WILLIAM CARLOS WILLIAMS "Young Woman at a Window" "Nantucket" "The Red Wheelbarrow" from Collected Poems Vol. 1, 1909-1939. Copyright 1938 by New Directions Publishing Corporation. Reprinted by permission of New Directions Publishing Corporation.

WILLIAM BUTLER YEATS "The Second Coming" "An Irish Airman Foresees His Death" "Sailing to Byzantium" "On Being Asked for a War Poem" "When You Are Old" "The Lake Isle of Innisfree" is reprinted by permission of A P Watt Limited on behalf of Micheal B. Yeats and Macmillan London Ltd.

ROBERT ZEND "World's Shortest Pessimistic Poem" "A Chain of Haik" reprinted by permission of the author.

DALE ZIEROTH "The Hunters of the Deer" from Clearing: Poems from a Journey (Toronto: House of Anansi Press, 1973). Reprinted by permission.

Additional Acknowledgements

E.E. CUMMINGS "A poet is someone who feels . . . " (quotation) appeared originally in the Ottawa Hills *Spectator* and is reprinted from *A Miscellany*, edited by George James Firmage, with permission of Liveright Publishing Corporation. Copyright 1955 by E.E. Cummings. Copyright © 1965 by Marion Morehouse Cummings. Copyright © 1958, 1965 by George James Firmage. "mortals)" "!blac" reprinted from *Complete Poems, 1913-1962*, by E.E. Cummings, by permission of Liveright Publishing Corporation. Copyright © 1923, 1925, 1931, 1935, 1938, 1939, 1940, 1944, 1945, 1946, 1947, 1948, 1949, 1950, 1951 1952, 1953, 1954, 1955, 1956, 1957, 1958, 1959, 1960, 1961, 1962, by the Trustees for the E.E. Cummings Trust. Copyright © 1961, 1963, 1968 by Marion Morehouse Cummings.

CHRIS DE BURGH "The Vision" Lyrics and Music by Chris De Burgh. © 1986 RONDOR MUSIC (LONDON) LTD. (PRS). All Rights Administered in the U.S. and Canada by ALMO MUSIC CORP. (ASCAP). All Rights Reserved. International Copyright Secured.

SUZANNE VEGA "Small Blue Thing" Lyrics by Suzanne Vega. Copyright 1985 AGF Music Ltd./Waifersongs Ltd. Used By Permission - All Rights Reserved.

WILLIAM BUTLER YEATS "An Irish Airman Foresees His Death" "Sailing to Byzantium" "On Being Asked for a War Poem" "When You Are Old" "The Lake Isle of Innisfree" from *The Collected Poems of W.B. Yeats*. Reprinted by permission of A P Watt Limited on behalf of Michael B. Yeats and Macmillan London Ltd.

Permission to reprint copyrighted material is gratefully acknowledged. The publishers have made every effort to trace the source of materials appearing in this book. Information that will enable the publishers to rectify any error or omission will be welcomed.